Poole Central Library
Dolphin Centre
Poole BH15 1QE
Tel: 01202 262421

2 0 JUL 2013

Please return this item to any Poole library
by the due date.
Renew on (01202) 265200 or at
www.boroughofpoole.com/libraries

lib/0810

Few Western politicians or academics have tried to comprehend the reclusive and enigmatic peninsula of Korea, known in history as the hermit kingdom. That long history, one of conquest, humiliation, and systematic abuse of human rights, parallels the worst experiences in Europe.

David Alton, and his fellow crusader Baroness Carline Cox, have visited North Korea several times, questioned and challenged its leadership, learned about the terrible record of its prison camps, its tortures, its induced famines over the course of sixty years, and met many witnesses to the extraordinary survival of faith, generosity of spirit, and forgiveness in the darkest places on earth. That evidence inspires them to believe there are ways out of this human hell. There are recent miracles in politics, David Alton reminds us – the bloodless transformation of South Africa from apartheid to democracy, the peaceful reunification of Germany. Given willingness in the United States and China to work together and to think out of the cage of the cold war, such a miracle could occur in the Korean peninsula, ending the world's nightmare of a North Korea willing to destroy on a nuclear scale to defend its regime. This is a book about brutality on a global scale. But it is also a book about hope.

Shirley Williams – Baroness Williams of Crosby

Building Bridges is destined to be the "Go-To" book on the world's most secretive nation by the Wilberforce of our time. This is an enthralling book that draws back the veil on North Korea's hidden world with a panoramic sweep of history, politics, and its Christian tradition. It is gripping, authoritative, accessible, and told with researcher's detail while revealing the personal courage of Gulag survivors. It also brings forth heroes of the faith such as the exciting rescue of Kim Dae-jung. David Alton isn't someone who delivers dispatches from a high tower but engages personally with people and issues, and his visits to North Korea (with Baroness Caroline Cox) add a valuable dimension. Bridges not Walls has been a theme of David Alton's work and this latest book shows that he leads the way with compelling insight into understanding North Korea but also to finding a window for the country to take its place in the world. "To begin is half the journey" is the title of one chapter. This book will help anyone intrigued by this mysterious nation to do just that.

Danny Smith, Jubilee Campaign

DAVID ALTON
& ROB CHIDLEY

BUILDING BRIDGES

IS THERE HOPE FOR NORTH KOREA?

FOREWORD BY BARONESS CAROLINE COX

LION

Published by Lion Books
an imprint of
Lion Hudson plc
Wilkinson House, Jordan Hill Road,
Oxford OX2 8DR, England
www.lionhudson.com

ISBN 978 0 7459 5598 8
e-ISBN 978 0 7459 5768 5

First edition 2013

Acknowledgments
Scripture quotations are taken from the *New Jerusalem Bible*
Copyright © 1985 by Darton, Longman & Todd and Les Editions du Cerf

A catalogue record for this book is available
from the British Library

Printed and bound in the UK, April 2013, LH26

Contents

Preface

When David Alton first asked me if I would be willing to read the manuscript of this book and write a preface to it my instant response was: "Why don't you get someone who knows North Korea to do it?" "That is just the problem", he responded, "it is difficult to find anyone in the public eye who knows North Korea!" Point taken. Having now read the book I must admit that to me and to so many politicians, North Korea really is a far away country of which we know nothing.

What David Alton and Rob Chidley have done is first give us a fascinating and eminently readable account of Korean history. The earlier parts were completely unknown to me and even the Korean War – its causes and outcomes – were but a hazy memory. Then they describe the conditions inside North Korea, together with the long stand-off with South Korea; since no peace treaty has been signed they remain technically at war. It is an absurdity not helped by South Korea's greatest ally, the United States.

The authors are unsparing in their graphic description of life inside North Korea and especially the gulag prison camps. Yet they convincingly argue for constructive dialogue and food aid to open up that country. There were times in our recent past when it was difficult to envisage the reunification of Germany, the end of apartheid in South Africa, peace and coalition government in Northern Ireland, or democracy breaking out in Burma. Yet these things have come to pass, and so their thesis that one day the 38th parallel could be a mere signpost is not so fanciful. This is an instructive volume about one of the world's most intractable and inscrutable trouble spots; but it bristles with faith and hope that a better life is possible for all who at present suffer in the isolation of North Korea. For that reason alone it is a most valuable read.

David Steel – Lord Steel of Aikwood

Acknowledgments

*This book is dedicated to the
people of Korea – who have endured much suffering
with great dignity and courage.*

In particular, David Alton would like to thank:

Professor Jae Won and the Law Department at Handong University; Ambassador Karen Wolstenholme, her predecessors, and the dedicated staff at the British Embassy in Pyongyang; Caroline (Baroness) Cox; Fiona Bruce MP; Jim Dobbin MP; Elizabeth (Baroness) Berridge; Lord Bates; Gary Streeter MP and the other officers of the All-Party Parliamentary Group on North Korea and its hon. clerk Keith Bennett; David Campanale and Chris Rogers of BBC World; Mark Rowland, James Mawdsley, Ben Rogers, and Sam Burke, who at different times all accompanied me to North Korea; Ambassadors Choo Kyu Ho and Lee Tae-sik of the Republic of Korea and Ambassadors Ri Yong Ho and Ja Song-nam of the DPRK, all unfailingly courteous and constructive; Xuelin, Lady Bates; John Lee; Justin Choi; Alice Choi; Luke de Pulford for his organization of the visit of the incoming delegation of the North Korean Speaker, Choe Tae-bok; Ann Buwalda and Danny Smith of Jubilee Campaign for their consistent encouragement and promotion of human rights and human dignity; John Kennedy CBE and Bill Hampson; Assemblywoman A. Young Lee and her husband C.J. Kim; Dr L.U. Kim; Dr James Kim; Fr Gerry Hammond; Cardinal Nicolas Cheong, Fr Hugo Park and the Archdiocese of Seoul; the Kim Dae-jung Presidential Library and Museum; the House of Lords Library – always helpful and patient; Shin Dong-hyok, whose story I relate, and for whom I have unending admiration; and Yoo Sang-joon, whose visit to the Westminster

Parliament in 2003, at which he recounted the loss of his entire family, provoked my interest in North Korea, and whose bravery, suffering, and dignity are representative of the Korean people I have been privileged to meet; Rob Chidley for his perseverance and professionalism in bringing this idea to publication, and Ali Hull at Lion, who commissioned and edited the manuscript; my four children who never cease to surprise and amaze me, and their mother, Lizzie, who has been a source of encouragement to me throughout.

Rob Chidley would like to thank:
Ali Hull, Caroline Masom, Jan Greenough, Ella Blackmore, Lucy Blackmore, and Richard Chidley.

Foreword

North Korea is perhaps the world's most closed nation, and one of the world's most under-reported and misunderstood. When it does feature on the international agenda, in the media or in the minds of policy-makers, it tends to be owing to concerns about security on the Korean peninsula, North Korea's nuclear programme, or questions about its dynastic leadership. Very rarely do the grave human rights and humanitarian concerns receive attention. Indeed, the severity of the suffering of the North Korean people is almost equally matched by the scale of ignorance or, worse, lack of interest shown by the outside world.

For over a decade, David Alton has been at the forefront of efforts to change this, and to put North Korea on the agenda of policy-makers, parliamentarians, the media, and the general public. He has been tireless in his advocacy of what could be called "Helsinki with a Korean face" – a need to be more creative in our approach to North Korea, to seek constructive, critical engagement, and to find ways, through dialogue and exchange, of opening up mindsets and challenging propaganda, rather than keeping the country isolated.

It has been my privilege to work with him in this endeavour, to travel together to Pyongyang on three occasions, and to share in a passionate belief that it is better to build bridges, not walls. That does not mean, for one moment, that we compromise our values or endorse the regime's appalling violations of human rights. Indeed, quite the opposite: it means putting our concerns about human rights firmly on the table, talking face to face with the regime, and looking its leadership in the eye. It means offering a hand of true friendship to the North Korean people. It means presenting the regime with alternative ways of doing things, challenging their own propaganda, and exposing them to the idea of freedom. On our most recent visit, one of the books we gave to officials in the regime was Karl Popper's *The Open Society and Its Enemies* (Routledge, 1945). It is only through such human contact, such critical, constructive engagement, that we have a chance of opening up such a closed society.

This book is a vital contribution to the effort to understand North Korea. Meticulously researched and engagingly written, it provides a detailed account of the history of the Korean peninsula, and an excellent analysis of the issues of paramount concern today: the gulags, the food shortages, the security issues, and the need to end the war and establish a lasting peace. David Alton and Rob Chidley offer a clear and insightful survey of the past, including the many periods in which the Korean people across the peninsula have suffered under occupation, war, and dictatorship. The influence of Christianity, with its stories of persecution and martyrdom, is a significant thread. The devastation of the Korean War, and the decades of tension, conflict, and division that have followed, are themes well documented by the authors.

But this is not just a history book. Understanding Korea's history is essential for comprehending the present and developing solutions for the future. David Alton and Rob Chidley provide some detailed ideas on how the international community should respond to the continuing crisis in Korea, and the solutions they put forward are ones that I strongly support. I hope that every reader, whether a diplomat, a journalist, an academic, a politician, an activist, an aid worker or an interested individual, will seriously consider their response to the evidence and the ideas presented in this book, and will engage in reaching out to the Korean people, North and South, to help to build bridges, tear down walls, and contribute towards a new era of justice, peace, and freedom.

Caroline Cox – The Baroness Cox of Queensbury
Chief Executive of HART and Vice-Chairman
of the All-Party Group on North Korea

How Do You Solve a Problem like Korea?

"There is – only a wall. And its bricks are laid on a mortar of lies… There is no law. The same treacherous secrecy, the same fog of injustice, still hangs in our air, worse than the smoke of city chimneys. For half a century and more the enormous state has towered over us, girded with hoops of steel. The hoops are still there. There is no law."

Alexander Solzhenitsyn, *The Gulag Archipelago* (1973)

After hearing me on BBC Radio Four's *Today* programme putting the case for constructive but critical engagement with North Korea, Tam Dalyell, the former Labour Member of Parliament and one-time "Father of the House of Commons", sent me a short note of encouragement. He recalled how, in the early 1950s, he and his friends had been called up to do National Service. He had been sent to Germany with the British Army of the Rhine (BAOR) while his friends had been sent to the Korean peninsula. None of them returned.

Around 1,000 British servicemen died in the Korean War – more than in Afghanistan, Iraq, and the Falklands combined. Millions of Koreans and thousands of Chinese and Americans perished. Yet, for many, this is a forgotten war – and one which, 60 years later, remains unresolved.

For the sake of those who died, and out of a deep desire to do all that is humanly possible to prevent the recurrence of such a terrible hemorrhaging of life, we all must play our part in working to end the war and put to rest the division of Korea.

At the end of the Korean War, a militarized wall was erected at the 38th Parallel, separating a single nation into two states, dividing family members from one another, and leaving brother estranged from brother.

Since then, ideologies, fear, and more modern and deadlier military hardware have added new layers of fortification to the wall.

In 2003, after making a highly critical speech in Parliament about human rights abuses in the North, I visited the Democratic People's Republic of Korea (DPRK) in the company of my colleague and good friend, Baroness (Caroline) Cox. I have since returned on three other occasions and have also travelled to the Tumen River, which separates North Korea from North-East China, to see where many Koreans have lost their lives trying to escape their homeland.

However scathing one might be about the country's political ideology and policies, it is hard not to be captivated by the Korean people, their culture, and their history. The pain of the separation reminded me of other walls that men have made – both metaphorical and real – in Berlin, South Africa, the Middle East, and Northern Ireland.

When Caroline and I travelled from Pyongyang to Panmunjom, where the 1953 Armistice was signed, the futility of Korea's wall, and the continued pain and danger that it represents, were not far from my mind.

Panmunjom is an uninhabited village that lies between North and South Korea. There, in a visitors' book in a featureless building overlooking the most fortified border in the world, I wrote: "It's better for men to build bridges than to build walls."

It seemed very apt for our surroundings.

I remain convinced that this is true, but I do not approach this subject from a well-meaning but naïve point of view. I simply believe we have been pursuing the wrong answers when confronted with the question "How do you solve a problem like Korea?"

The two central propositions in this book are that it is time to end the war on the Korean peninsula – both technically and in reality – and that we must use our skills and genius to build bridges between North Korea and the world.

Building a wall requires little genius or engineering know-how. Bridges, by contrast, are more challenging, more complex, and ultimately more freeing – though they do have the disadvantage of being walked over. Perhaps that's why violent military confrontation sometimes seems more attractive than the back-and-forth of genuine dialogue. For those who do not experience the human cost of violence and division, opting for the clarity of conflict must seem easier because it requires less patience, persistence, and effort.

Dialogue, however, should not become an excuse for appeasement or for timidity in speaking truthfully about the nature of a regime, its ideology, and its policies. Despite our failings, we who share a common belief in human rights, human dignity, and freedom must be fearless in confronting the brutality and ruthlessness of those who do not ascribe to a recognizable humanitarian belief.

North Korea is, in many ways, the victim-turned-perpetrator of systematized abuse. As this book relates, the Korean people suffered terribly under the humiliating Japanese occupation in the run-up to the Second World War. Following VJ Day and the Armistice of 15 August 1945, the Korean nation went into shock, once again effectively occupied by foreign forces. As the Allies attempted to hand over power to an indigenous Korean government, the Communists in the north (under Russian-trained guerrilla fighter Kim Il-sung) broke off all meaningful engagement. Five years later, North Korea re-engaged with its southern neighbour in a terrifying manner – down the barrels of the guns of advancing Soviet-supplied tanks.

What followed was a conflict as futile and bloody as any other in modern history, in which more bombs fell on the Korean peninsula than were dropped within the Pacific theatre in the Second World War.[1]

Though the vast majority of the shelling stopped with the ceasefire of 27 July 1953, the war is, contrary to popular impression, still ongoing – no peace treaty was signed. Instead of "hot" conflict, the war became a nervous stand-off as part of the worldwide Cold War. Though the USSR fell and the international Cold War ended, it still lingers on in the Korean peninsula. The tragedy has also lingered; 60 years of austerity, failed self-reliance, and famine have passed and the North Korean people still suffer in unimaginable ways.

Recognizing the unacceptable reality of such cruelty and abuse is a necessary part of understanding North Korea today. Chapter 10 contains harrowing subject matter that is difficult to read, but we must face the enormity of what is occurring. The DPRK leadership must acknowledge it too, so, if we are to firmly force that issue into the dialogue, we must face it ourselves. If we do not, we cannot hope for real change.

---

1. "The US Air Force estimated that North Korea's destruction was proportionately greater than that of Japan in the Second World War, where the US had turned 64 major cities to rubble and used the atomic bomb to destroy two others. American planes dropped 635,000 tons of bombs on Korea – that is, essentially on North Korea – including 32,557 tons of napalm, compared to 503,000 tons of bombs dropped in the entire Pacific theatre of World War II." From *The Asia-Pacific Journal: Japan Focus* http://www.japanfocus.org/-charles_k_-armstrong/3460 Originally cited in *A Substitute for Victory: The Politics of Peacemaking at the Korean Armistice Talks* by Rosemary Foot (Ithaca: Cornell University Press, 1990), pp. 207–208.

Thankfully, there are opportunities for change, if not actual signs. "Marshal" Kim Jong-un, the grandson of "Dear Leader" Kim Il-sung, is now in power and has yet to prove what kind of leader he will be. His uncle, Jang Sung-taek, has been working with him to make some small but welcome economic changes. But this is a dynastic system and Kim Jong-un is now in charge. Although he will be wary of radical change and in no sense is his leadership a reason for celebration in itself, his Western education, his youth, and his knowledge of other ways of doing things certainly represent a stylistic change. His father was recorded as uttering only six words in public in 19 years; he has already demonstrated that he knows how to speak and knows how to use modern media. All of this offers new possibilities.

It is therefore an opportune time for a fresh wave of engagement with the Hermit Kingdom in the north of the Korean peninsula. Change is in the air throughout the region and the world. Barack Obama has won his second term as president of the United States and South Korea has picked Park Geun-hye to be its first female president. There is also change in Japan and a significant transfer of power in China – from Hu Jintao to Xi Jinping. All of this marks a real opportunity for a new generation of leaders to make progress.

China's role will be crucial. President Xi Jinping studied economics at North Korea's Kim Il-sung University and knows the country well. He believes it is crucial to stabilize North Korea and to halt its nuclear ambitions.

More important still is the economic power China has over North Korea[2] and the fact that China is putting pressure on North Korea to open itself up to the world and reform. On a number of occasions in the recent past, China is said to have temporarily closed down its vital oil supply to North Korea

2. In 2005 52 per cent of North Korea's trade was with China. By 2011 it was 84 per cent, and 90 per cent of North Korea's crude oil comes from China.

as a form of leverage. China can exert significant influence to encourage North Korea to reform.

There is every hope that the North Korean people may one day enjoy the political and social freedom of their southern neighbours. The dream of emancipation may not be so far off. Only decades ago, South Korea struggled under the boot of a tyrant. In the 1980s, as the oppressive Park Chung-hee regime clamped down on dissident voices in South Korea, Cardinal Stephen Kim described "the long dark tunnel of dictatorship" that the church would have to endure if it were to speak truth and justice to the Korean people. "Great courage" would be needed, he said.

Cardinal Kim's resolve was tested in 1987 when pro-democracy students took refuge in Seoul's Myeongdong Cathedral. When ordered to hand them over to the authorities, he responded in trenchant terms: "If the police break into the cathedral, I will be in the very front. Behind me, there will be reverends and nuns. After we are wrestled down, there will be students."

It was the breaking point of the dictatorship. To get the students, they would have had to use military force against the Cardinal Archbishop of Seoul, whose own grandfather had died in the religious persecutions, who himself in his youth had been antagonistic to the Japanese occupation, and who was a hero in his own right to many, many people. The military junta in the South then faltered and unravelled.

Sometimes there comes a singular moment when all it takes is one person to stand up and oppose tyranny, even at great personal cost.

Cardinal Kim's stand reminded me of a similar, if more widely known, opponent of injustice who saw his country overcome division and oppression. Nobel Peace Laureate Archbishop Desmond Tutu confronted the power of the state in circumstances similar to those facing Cardinal Kim, as writer and activist Jim Wallis relates:

I was there in Cape Town in [Tutu's] cathedral when the place was surrounded by soldiers and police who outnumbered the worshippers three to one. He looked at them and pointed his finger and said, "You are very powerful, but you are not gods. And I serve a God who cannot be mocked. You have already lost, so I invite you today to come and join the winning side!"[3]

Wallis continues:

Later, I was at the inauguration of Nelson Mandela, and I said, "Bishop, do you remember what you said that morning?" He smiled. I said, "Today, they've joined the winning side."

Dr Martin Luther King, paraphrasing the abolitionist preacher Theodore Parker, said that "the arc of the moral universe is long, but it bends toward justice". The bend of the arc seems particularly long for Korea, but justice may be just around the corner.

There are precedents for remarkable change within countries under even the most oppressive and nightmarish dictatorships. A better future for North Korea is imaginable, if only the international and domestic powers can rise above their vested interests and grasp the opportunity. There will, of course, need to be a significant movement within North Korea too. For change to be sustained, it must come from within Korea. This does not absolve us of any involvement – indeed, there remains a burden on us to help support, encourage, and equip the next generation of Stephen Kims to stand up for the Korean people.

Throughout the Cold War, alliances were formed between dissidents, religious leaders, democrats, and human rights

3. "The Gospel is personal, but never private", Homiletics Interview. http://www.homileticsonline.com/subscriber/interviews/wallis.asp

activists. In 1975, at Helsinki, the principles of critical engagement, dialogue, strong deterrence of attempted aggression, and insistence on respect for human rights began a process that ended in the fall of the Iron Curtain. Looking out over the fortified walls of Panmunjom, I could not help but notice many parallels between the end of the Cold War and the situation in North Korea today.

On returning from one of my visits, in a debate in the House of Lords, I argued:

> *By championing the cause of those who are suffering in North Korea, the international community will create the conditions for the establishment of democracy... Learning the lessons of [the] Helsinki [process], we must do nothing to license the regime in Pyongyang to commit further atrocities against its own people. We should enter negotiations which guarantee human rights, such as free exchange of people and religious liberties... By linking the present crisis with the human rights violations, a crisis can be turned into an opportunity. To do nothing about North Korea would be the most dangerous option of all.*

"Helsinki with a Korean face" is a cause which Baroness Cox and I have championed since our visits to North Korea. American North Korea expert David Hawk said of a Helsinki-style engagement with North Korea: "It is the approach that has yet to be tried."[4]

It is worth pursuing – for all the world.

---

4. "Pursuing Peace While Advancing Rights: The Untried Approach to North Korea", May 2010.

CHAPTER 1

Where Confucius Was King

On Baekdu Mountain, myths are born. The broad amphitheatre of steep brown rock encircles more than just an iris-blue crater lake; it holds the identity of a people bound up in legend. Korean folklore tells that it was at Baekdu Mountain, now on the border between North Korea and China, that the Divine Prince Hwanung, son of the Heavenly Emperor Hwanin, stepped down to earth with 3,000 followers to establish the perfect kingdom. He founded Sinsi, the City of God, and ruled every aspect of life with great wisdom and power.

Before long, so the legend has it, a tigress and a bear that lived on the mountain petitioned Hwanung to give them human form. He promised to grant their wish on condition that they remain inside a nearby cave for 100 days with only garlic and mugwort for food. The animals took up the challenge and began their vigil. The impatient tigress soon yearned to roam the mountains and became hungry for food more satisfying than herbs, so she left the cave in search of prey. The bear persisted without complaint and, after 100 days, she emerged from the darkness of the cave as a beautiful woman called Ungnyeo.

Though she became lovelier every day, Ungnyeo also grew lonely and longed for a baby to comfort her. Hwanung heard of her sorrow and he married her and gave her a son. The child was called Dangun, the Altar Prince, and is revered as the founder of the Korean people. Dangun ascended the throne and called his kingdom *Chosŏn*,[5] meaning "the land of morning

---

5. Later referred to as Ancient Chosŏn with the advent of the second Chosŏn dynasty in AD 1392.

freshness", and in 2333 BC, so the myth maintains, he founded the city of Asadal – now Pyongyang, the capital of North Korea.

Exactly 4,275 years later, in 1942, another birth supposedly took place on the slopes of Baekdu Mountain. According to officials of the Democratic People's Republic of Korea (DPRK), Supreme Leader Kim Jong-il was born at a secret location on the mountainside. His birth was heralded by a swallow and, as he was born, a new star appeared in the sky and a double rainbow was seen over the mountaintop.

The reality was not nearly so fantastical: Kim Jong-il was actually born on 16 February 1941 in the Russian village of Vyatskoye, on the banks of the Amur River, where his father, Kim Il-sung, commanded the 1st Battalion of the Soviet 88th Brigade. Kim Jong-il only set foot on the Korean mainland as a little boy in the November of 1945 after the Second World War had ended and Korea had regained its independence from Japan.

It was no accident that the DPRK's propagandists claimed a connection between Kim Jong-il and the mountain. For over four millennia, the people of the Korean peninsula had viewed Baekdu Mountain as their spiritual origin and a wellspring of human greatness. The legend of Kim Jong-il's divinely mandated birth may appear laughable to the cynical Western reader, but not so to the culturally entrenched population of North Korea, who still believe that Kim Jong-il's birthday was celebrated across the world. Neither is it the only claim the modern Kim dynasty makes to the ancient Korean heritage. Kim Il-sung, the "Great Leader", supposedly led the resistance against occupying Japanese forces from a base in the thick forests that cover the slopes of this very significant mountain.

Korean scholars and citizens still trace their people's ancestry back to the first king, Dangun, and his Chosŏn kingdom, but the lineage is questionable. The disputed text *Gyuwon Sahwa*, written in 1675, describes ancient Korean history including the lineage of 47 Dangun leaders from 2333 to 1128 BC, but there is disagreement between historians on its historical reliability and exactly when the Chosŏn kingdom was founded.

There is, however, a broad consensus on the kingdom's development: it was one among many fortified towns that fought for supremacy, increasing in power over its neighbours through conquest or treaty. It was not until around 400 BC that a recognizable federation of walled city states emerged under a single king. Despite what the ancient legend might say, it was closer to 300 BC when the capital of the Chosŏn kingdom was moved to Pyongyang – it was certainly not done under the all-seeing eye of the first king, Dangun.

The Chosŏn kingdom survived until 108 BC, when its territory was invaded by the Han dynasty of China.[6] The old kingdom fractured quickly and reverted to individual city states which fought each other and outside invaders for survival. Over the next three centuries the smaller chiefdoms and confederacies were gradually absorbed into three dominant factions: the Koguryŏ, Baekje, and Silla kingdoms.

The northern Koguryŏ occupied vast swathes of land from central southern Korea to far into China. They were a people shaped by the hard, mountainous landscape and by an almost constant state of war on all fronts. They were formidable warriors, prizing both individual prowess and organized strategy, employing powerful bowmen and heavy cavalry.

Their greatest military victory came in AD 612 when the Sui dynasty of China mobilized over 1.1 million soldiers against them. Of this larger force, a division of 305,000 Chinese penetrated the Koguryŏ defensive line far enough to reach

---

6. The terms "China" and "Chinese" are not used for historical accuracy but rather for the convenience of the modern reader. They simply refer to the relevant dominant power originating in the territory that is today known as China.

Pyongyang, where they were lured into a bloody ambush by Koguryŏ General Eulji Mundeok. Of the original 305,000 men, only 2,700 lived to see their homeland again.

Not much is known about Koguryŏ culture, as many records have been lost, but we can infer much from their contact with other peoples. In addition to the warring arts, the Koguryŏ were masters of misinformation, at one time sending stone spearheads to China as tribute to avoid revealing their expertise in Iron Age weaponry. They were also learned and prized Confucian thought, even establishing *T'aehak*, a national Confucian university, in AD 372.

The Koguryŏ legacy was sufficiently useful to the DPRK leadership for a symposium to be held in North Korea in 2003 to celebrate the birthday of King Tongmyŏng, founder of the Koguryŏ kingdom. Speakers at Kim Jong-il's symposium all agreed that "the history of Koguryŏ proves that a country strong in combat power and developed in all spheres of social life can be a powerful nation free from flunkeyism, submission, and dependence on foreign forces."

To the south-west of Koguryŏ lay the Baekje kingdom. This land was excellent for cultivation but much of its produce was sent to China as tribute until the people sought closer diplomatic ties with Japan. Under pressure from Koguryŏ from the north and Silla from the east, Baekje retreated south, losing Seoul to Koguryŏ in AD 475. They established a new capital at Gongju in modern-day South Korea. Safe within the natural defence of the mountains, the Baekje capital was more secure from attack, but effectively cut off from the outside world.

The Baekje kings formed alliances both with and against their Silla and Koguryŏ neighbours alternately, switching their loyalty as need dictated. In AD 538 King Seong moved the capital to the more accessible city of Sabi, where the Baekje people blossomed, opening diplomatic and trade links with China and adopting more Buddhist teachings. The Baekje kingdom lasted until AD 660, when the allied forces of Silla and the Tang dynasty of China invaded, taking the capital, Sabi, and quickly annexing the entire Baekje territory.

In the east, the Silla dynasty began as a chiefdom in the walled city confederacies and grew to power, absorbing smaller states into itself. They were excellent warriors, preferring horseback archery to close combat. Silla fought with China against the Koguryŏ and also against numerous Baekje–Japanese alliances. In AD 668, just eight years after defeating Baekje, Silla crushed the weakened Koguryŏ and achieved the unification of the Korean peoples for the first time.

Silla existed for a remarkable 992 years and was ruled by three feuding royal families: the Park, Seok, and Kim clans. Each of the three royal clans claimed their own fantastical birth stories for their patriarchs. Kim Alji's legendary story describes his being born from a golden box found hanging from a tree in the forest with a white rooster crowing underneath it. The child glowed with wondrous light and so the ruler, King Talhae, raised him and named him *Kim*, meaning "golden". That the DPRK created a fantastical birth legend for Kim Jong-il was not only meant to signal continuity with the ancient royal Kim, but was also highly suggestive of their plans to establish a new Kim dynasty for a new Korea.

Even before the unification of Korea under the Silla dynasty, Confucianism had risen to prominence. In AD 682 Silla established *Kukh'ak*, another national Confucian college, and, after unification, the royal families of Silla adopted Confucian forms of governance to manage the nation and limit the power of the unruly aristocratic families. But Confucianism did not go unchallenged because, though Buddhism's influence was lessened in the political sphere, it still occupied a central place in the lives of the general population.

Confucianism was imported into Korea from China as both a code for living and a tool for administration and statecraft. It is a social, ethical, and political system that focuses on the relationship of the individual with wider society, and on how altruism (*rén*), moral behaviour (*yi*) and propriety (*li*) are to the benefit of all.

Though ritualistic, Confucianism lacked a deity and therefore did not compete with the local practice of folk religions, Shamanism, Buddhism, or Christianity in Korea. It was theologically non-threatening to the status quo. In addition, many tenets of Confucian thought are directly compatible with the beliefs and social practices of the major world religions. Though he was born over 500 years before Christ, Confucius summarized the Golden Rule thus: "Never impose on others what you would not choose for yourself."

Other Confucian teachings expressed ideas very close to biblical wisdom. Han Yu, a Chinese Confucian born in AD 768, wrote an essay beginning, "Widely extended kindness is called love; acts that move in line with truth are called righteousness; a life lived in accord with these is true religion." His teachings spread throughout the Silla kingdom and his work is strongly comparable with biblical texts such as James 1:27: "Pure, unspoilt religion, in the eyes of God our Father, is this: coming to the help of orphans and widows in their hardships, and keeping oneself uncontaminated by the world", and Micah 6:8: "You have already been told what is right and what Yahweh wants of you. Only this, to do what is right, to love loyalty and to walk humbly with your God."

Alongside these socially enlightened beliefs, Confucian "compatibility" with other religions had practical drawbacks. Praiseworthy Confucian tenets such as honouring one's elders and obeying one's teachers became entwined with shamanistic practices such as ancestor worship and deification.

Strong threads of Confucian thought can be identified in the psyche of the North Korean people today. It is arguable that the DPRK propagandists had an easier time establishing the veneration of Kim Il-sung and Kim Jong-il in the minds of the population because they could draw on the cultural marination of two millennia of Confucian thought tied up with ancestor deification and elder veneration. The behaviour of the distraught news anchor who sobbed through her announcement of Kim Jong-il's death in December 2011 is perhaps a little less incredible and more understandable in the light of this.

Similarly, one tenet of Confucian teaching regularly twisted by the DPRK is the "rectification of names". Two and a half millennia before George Orwell wrote *Nineteen Eighty-four*, Confucius recognized that social disorder often stemmed from failure to perceive, understand, and deal with reality – and that social reality was tied up with language. If one did not respect the use of language – or, worse, if one manipulated language and the meaning of words for selfish ends – chaos would follow. This has happened in North Korea. Six decades of adding the suffix *nom*, meaning "bastard", to anything or anyone American has had a powerful effect and calling all American leaders *gangpae*, meaning "gangster", does not make dialogue with the most powerful nation on earth very easy. At the other extreme, giving North Korea's starving, naked street children the name of *Khot-jebi*, meaning "flower swallows", does not make their destitution any more poetic.

The Confucian influence on the Korean people survived the fall of the Silla dynasty in AD 935, when the kingdom submitted to the newly established and energetic Koryŏ dynasty. It is from the word *Koryŏ*, which itself is rooted in the word for the older kingdom, *Koguryŏ*, that the modern word *Korea* is derived.

The Koryŏ capital was located at Songdo (modern-day Kaesŏng, just north of the 38th Parallel) and on a direct line between Pyongyang and Seoul. The city was a grand administrative centre with palaces, offices, and temples, but few markets or public entertainments. Songdo began as a symbol of government power rather than a city built for the people, and the business of the day involved strengthening the state and fighting off invasion from the north.

The Koryŏ people were ruled by puppet kings, manipulated by a succession of dictators from the corrupt and powerful Choe family. An envoy from China named Hsu Ching noted in AD 1123 that the elite in Koryŏ lived in splendour and enviable comfort, while the masses lived in misery. The Koryŏ court was embarrassed by this report and tried to hide the country's wider conditions from visitors. Civil unrest occurred frequently until AD 1231, when the Mongol hordes swept down onto the Korean peninsula from Russia.

The royal family surrendered immediately and Koryŏ became a vassal state of the Mongol Empire. Instead of sending sufficient tribute to the Mongol court, the royal family and the Choe household escaped with a vast hoard of treasure to Kwanghwa Island, just off the coast near Seoul. In response, the furious Mongols poured back onto the peninsula. Though they were the most formidable fighting force the world had ever seen, they were terrible sailors and could not make a successful landing on Kwanghwa Island. Instead, they satisfied themselves with forcibly extracting tribute from the impoverished peasants and, while the mainland burned, the Choe dictatorship and their royal puppets lived lives of unconcerned luxury.

In AD 1258, the Choe family changed its position regarding the Mongol power following the assassination of Choe Ui, the head of the ruling family. By way of apology, they sent Crown Prince Chungnyeol to the Mongol court to pledge Koryŏ's subservience. After this, Koryŏ experienced a period of relative peace and prosperity under Mongol vassalage, until the waning of Mongol power opened their shores to raiders and their borders to the rising power of Ming China.

Around AD 1360 Ming defeated the Mongol armies in southern China, reducing Mongol power over Korea. They followed up their victory with a letter to the Koryŏ court, instructing them that tribute was due. The court was divided over which power they should appease, but the brooding Mongol power extracted tribute by force and the relationship soured once again. But China was not a threat that could be ignored.

In AD 1388 the Koryŏ court ordered one of their most accomplished military commanders, Yi Songgye, to lead an army of over 500,000 soldiers against the Ming. Yi was a veteran commander and no coward, but he objected to this new task as hopeless, even impossible. As his army marched, his men deserted in droves and, when he reached the Yalu River (which marks the border between modern-day China and North Korea), he turned back. He marched instead on the Koryŏ capital of Songdo and overthrew the very rulers who had sent him against the Chinese. Yi took the name King Taejo, after two ancient and iconic Korean kings. He moved the capital city to modern-day Seoul and there established the second Chosŏn dynasty, which endured for over 500 years.

The first two centuries of the second Chosŏn dynasty's rule were relatively peaceful. They achieved this by carefully handling the crumbling Mongol power and appeasing the growing power of the Ming Chinese with the payment of tribute. Under these conditions, the dynasty achieved complete territorial occupation of the Korean peninsula and ushered in the golden age of Korean culture, trade, and science.

One of the greatest achievements of the era was the invention in 1443 of the Korean alphabet, known as *hangul*. Upon its creation, King Sejong did not lose the opportunity to emphasize the script's pure Korean heritage and that it was derived from neither the Japanese nor the Chinese script systems.[7]

But the blossoming of Korea brought threats and problems of its own. Within Korea itself, Chosŏn cultural development also instilled in the people a quasi-Confucian fatalism that would be easily manipulated 600 years later by the DPRK leadership: "The good man... asks no favours and makes no complaints, blaming neither God who dwells above nor his fellow man who sits below. The good man, therefore, accepts his place and awaits the will of Heaven." The will for societal and technological advancement faltered.[8]

In the region, the threat of invasion from neighbouring powers grew ever more real. Successive raids and provocations by foreign powers allowed Korean leaders to make political gains by promoting isolationism and the rejection of everything foreign. Combining this with its stagnating technological development, Korea weakened itself and pushed its allies away.

For almost 100 years following the 1498 political purges under King Yeonsangun, the Chosŏn court disintegrated into numerous warring factions. As each group rose in power, it committed atrocities upon its rivals and inspired yet more vengeful acts as the political fortunes changed. Accusations of treason and subsequent executions became a common political tactic and, by 1590, Korea was a weak, backward, and divided nation.

Japan sensed an opportunity.

---

7. This beautiful and ingenious lettering system is still the official script of both North and South Korea.

8. Not all Confucians opposed external influences and technological development; *Silhak*, meaning "practical learning", was a Confucian reform movement spanning the seventeenth, eighteenth, and nineteenth centuries, designed to counter the stifling influence of the dominant philosophy. This outward-looking progressive movement called for relief for the plight of peasant classes and technological exchange with other nations. Unfortunately, most of the proponents were outside the power structures of government and had little influence at court. The movement failed.

CHAPTER 2

Under Japanese Rule

In May 1592, the ambitious samurai general Hideyoshi landed over 150,000 men on the south-eastern tip of the Korean peninsula. It was the largest successful amphibious landing in history, until D-Day 352 years later, and the Japanese troops came with two objectives: to obliterate the state of Korea and to use the peninsula as a springboard into China.

Many years before, Toyotomi Hideyoshi had risen from the peasantry to become a powerful general through distinguished service to the warlord Oda Nobunaga. Until his death, Nobunaga had pursued his vision of an all-conquering Japan united under the Divine Emperor, and Hideyoshi took on his mentor's dream. Though he fought tirelessly to defeat the dissenting warlords and suppress rebellion, Nobunaga did not live to see his dream realized; he had to leave it to his trusted ally Hideyoshi to achieve it.

Hideyoshi quickly began subduing dissenting Japanese clans and his power grew. In 1585 he was named Regent by the Emperor's court and became the recognized ruler of Japan. Finally, in 1590, he defeated the last opposing warlords and achieved complete unification of his country. With the full support of Japan's fearsome warrior clans, he turned his eye across the waters towards his Chosŏn neighbours and Ming China beyond. He planned to sweep the Korean kingdom aside and use the "rice bowl" peninsula as a stepping stone towards his true goal of China. Within two years, his army was rearmed and ready.

The landing of Hideyoshi's army in 1592 took three full days and nights to achieve. He brought with him the world's most feared fighters – his veteran samurai warriors. Not only were they armed with their renowned *daishō* and *tachi* swords, they also carried the world's most advanced weapon: the arquebus firearm, forerunner of the musket.

In better times, Japanese diplomats had actually presented the Chosŏn court with a number of arquebuses with which they might have revolutionized their armies, but the knee-jerk reaction of isolationism meant the court had failed to recognize the power of these weapons. In combat the Chosŏn soldiers paid a heavy price. They had access to primitive hand cannon firearms, but these were almost useless against the more modern technology. Instead, they had to rely on the superior range of arrows fired from powerful composite bows, but they could not match the firepower of the Japanese forces or withstand the terrifying blur of peerless swordsmanship at close quarters. The Chosŏn soldiers fled.

Most of the peninsula was quickly conquered, including the cities of Seoul, Kaesŏng, and Pyongyang. The Chosŏn court fled north, petitioning their Chinese overlords for help, but Ming China was slow to react. It was only because of the tactical brilliance of the Korean Admiral Yi Sun-sin that Korea was not annexed then. The Korean navy was as formidable at sea as the Japanese army was on land. Years of repelling the savage Wakō pirate raiders from the coasts of Korea had trained Admiral Yi and his men in the unforgiving arts of naval combat. He also commanded a navy equipped with the most advanced hardware in the world, armour-plated *panokseon* war galleys of Korean origin, which bristled with long-range cannons that were capable of firing exploding shells.

Though outnumbered, Admiral Yi was anything but outgunned or outranged, and could attack with impunity. He obliterated the opposing armada, severing the Japanese army's supply lines and forcing their withdrawal. In doing so, Yi saved the country but doomed the population. The starving Japanese army pillaged as they retreated, leaving farms burned, barns empty, workers slaughtered, and women raped. With an allied Korean–Chinese army advancing from the north, and little hope of escape via ship to the south, the Japanese army eventually sued for peace. The bloodshed ended, but famine followed the destruction and the impoverished Korean people perished in their tens of thousands.

With so many civilians dead, kidnapped, or enslaved, and so many cultural artefacts destroyed or looted, the Chosŏn court was forced to face the long-ignored need to reform its military. It rearmed and retrained its armies and instituted the universal draft into armed service. This included slaves and men from the upper classes for the first time, and the reforms ensured that every man of fighting age was proficient in the use of weapons – including the modern arquebus.

When Hideyoshi landed 141,000 men in Korea again in 1597, he found a better-organized Korean defence and a China eager to respond more quickly to their vassal's call for help. This time China was not Hideyoshi's ultimate goal; instead, the subjugation and humiliation of the Korean people was all he sought. By the end of 1598, an estimated 1 million people lay dead and the Korean mainland was devastated once more. Japan failed to conquer the peninsula and neither Hideyoshi nor Admiral Yi survived the conflict.

China had honoured its obligation to protect its vassal state, but the price paid was high. Japan, though torn apart by internal strife in the aftermath of the failure of the second invasion, benefited in the long term from the artistic and cultural advances stolen along with thousands of Korean abductees. The ordinary Korean people suffered worst from famine, disease, and brutality at the hands of both their Japanese enemies and their Chinese allies. Hatred for Japan and all things foreign swelled in all sections of society and the impulse towards isolationist policies calcified in the bones of the ruling classes.

Relations did not improve over the following centuries as Korea shut its doors and snubbed every Japanese envoy that petitioned for access. By the 1870s, factions in the Japanese court were lobbying for a punitive expedition against Korea to punish them for a perceived disrespect for the Divine Emperor of Japan. Though no warships were launched, Japan succeeded in opening three Korean ports to trade (and espionage) and, after Japanese diplomats were murdered in an attempted internal Korean coup, Japan leveraged the right to station troops on the Korean mainland to protect their diplomatic officials.

Under the weakened Chosŏn dynasty, opposing groups within the political establishment attempted their own coups with the aid of foreign military powers. In the following years of unrest, Korea became an exercise yard for the Chinese and Japanese militaries, as both nations backed different warring factions in the fracturing Korean government. Japan succeeded in ending Korea's vassalage by defeating Chinese forces in the First Sino-Japanese War, which lasted nine months from the summer of 1894 to the spring of 1895. The result was a greater concentration of Japanese troops stationed in Korea, and resentment of anything Japanese became ever more deeply ingrained in the Korean people.

Chosŏn Queen Min was an ardent critic of Japanese expansion, so much so that the Japanese court considered her an obstacle worth removing. When efforts to discredit her failed, assassins broke into the royal compound in late 1895 and butchered the queen and two of her attendants. They burned her body in a nearby forest and scattered the remains. Little was done about the murder, except for a show trial in Japan which found the accused assassins and their alleged backers not guilty because of a lack of evidence.

The outraged Korean people reacted by forming armed militias called "Righteous Armies" and baying for Japanese blood. By contrast, King Gojong fled to the safety of the Russian legation in Seoul for his own protection from assassination by other Japanese agents. The Chosŏn royals were desperate and running out of options. Russian interest in Korea had grown steadily in recent decades and now the Korean court leaned towards them for protection against the hated Japanese.

By 1897, having narrowly avoided being overrun by Japan and still under immense pressure from a number of foreign powers, the Chosŏn court declared King Gojong to be Emperor Gwangmu of "the Great Korean Empire". It was an effort to reassert national integrity and appease the powerful anti-Japanese sentiment that pervaded all sections of society, but it could do nothing to prevent the seemingly inevitable encroachment of Japanese power.

Unfortunately for the helpless Chosŏn and their demoralized subjects, the defeat of the Russian Empire by Japan in the Russo-Japanese war of 1904–05 ended all hope of independence, and Korea was left with no ally to hide behind.

In 1905 Korea was declared an imperial Japanese protectorate. Five years later, on 29 August 1910, to the humiliation of the Korean people, Japan deposed the royal family and annexed Korea by force. Korean hatred for Japan was immense, but the nation's power and sovereignty had been utterly crushed.

Japanese migrants had been settling in Korea for decades before annexation. By 1910, there were over 170,000 on the peninsula and they were hungry for land and opportunity. The new government seized land from Korean farmers and sold it at discounted rates to Japanese settlers. The traditional Korean land-ownership system was also reformed from a verbal or familial agreement to a written registry. As there were no written records to prove ownership, Korean families who had worked the same land for centuries were automatically dispossessed. Many of the foreign settlers set punitive tax rates for their tenants, often exacting as much as half of the food crop. This deepened both the poverty and the resentment among their Korean workforce. The result was a steady migration of Korean nationals from the farms to the cities, where dangerous factory work and prostitution were often the only immediate means of earning an income. With fewer workers in the fields and unmanageably high taxes on food production, famine returned to Korea.

The fomenting anger found expression on 1 March 1919 when a group of Korean nationalists gathered in Seoul to read the Korean declaration of independence and deliver a list of complaints to the Japanese government. The "March First Movement", as it became known, was triggered in part by the alleged assassination of the deposed Emperor Gojong in January of the same year. The complaints centred on the issues of heavy taxes, forced labour, unequal education, and lack of fairness in the treatment of Japanese and Korean citizens. The nationalists were arrested and immediately imprisoned. Mass demonstrations followed and the Japanese police responded with deadly force.

Park Eunsik, later the leader of the exiled provisional government of the Republic of Korea, reported that over 7,500 people were killed, 15,000 wounded, and 46,000 arrested. Many of those arrested were tortured and executed without trial in Seoul's notorious Seodaemun Prison.

The Japanese authorities took control of the news media in an effort to redirect emerging Korean nationalism and "re-educate" the population. Korean newspapers such as the *Chosun Ilbo* (Korea Daily News) were allowed to continue publication in opposition to the government, but were subjected to regular suspensions and sanctions whenever anti-Japanese sentiments were overtly expressed. The first time was on 27 August 1920, when the paper published an editorial that exposed the brutal treatment of Korean citizens at the hands of the Japanese police.

The editor and publisher of the *Chosun Ilbo* were regularly arrested and pressured to take a more sympathetic editorial stance towards Japan. Between 1920 and 1932 the paper was suspended four times and had over 500 separate editions confiscated because of Japanese displeasure. Subsequently, the paper took a more collaborative approach to the occupying powers but the suspensions and prohibitions had taken their toll. The paper finally closed in 1940 because of bankruptcy and government interference.[9]

It was not only the press that was censored. The Korean education system was replaced with Japanese imperial education, promoting a version of history in which Japan was the centre of artistic culture, progressive thought, technological excellence, and societal brilliance. Korea, by contrast, was portrayed as a backward, primitive society crying out for modernization and intervention from their benevolent Asiatic neighbours. Korean literature was even rewritten in praise of the Emperor of Japan.

Alongside the "re-education" of the Korean population, the Japanese authorities implemented a policy of cultural rewriting. Over 100,000 ancient artefacts from all periods of Korean history were excavated and removed, many into private collections in Japan. Part of the iconic Gyeongbokgung Palace, built by the second Chosŏn dynasty, was demolished to make way for the Japanese General Government Building. Other landmarks, such as prominent statues and temple carvings, were moved to new locations in order to fit the new historical narrative that the foundational Baekje and Silla kingdoms were part-Japanese in origin. The cultural and historical appropriation was designed to justify every attempt at Japanese colonization of the peninsula,

---

9. After independence in 1945 the *Chosun Ilbo* resumed publication, free of colonial censorship and suppression.

from the failed invasion of 1592 to the successful Annexation Treaty of 1910.

Even the beautiful and eminently practical Korean lettering system, *hangul*, was banned from use. This phonetic alphabet, dating from the fifteenth century, was uniquely Korean and was as much a symbol of the Chosŏn golden age – and therefore of Korean identity – as it was a lettering system.

Dissent and active resistance were dealt with in the most severe manner. Many former soldiers from the disbanded Korean army fled north, forming resistance groups to harass and frustrate further Japanese expansion. Villages accused of harbouring such resistance fighters were often razed to the ground and their inhabitants slaughtered. Typical tactics, as reported by a number of eyewitnesses, included herding the entire population of a village into a single building, which was then locked, surrounded, set on fire, and peppered with bullets.

Japan's appetite for territorial expansion remained unsatisfied. In September 1931, the Mukden Incident (also known as the Manchurian Incident) was the first of many engineered disputes designed to provoke China into what became the Second Sino-Japanese War, finally declared in July 1937. By December 1937, Nanking, the former capital of the Republic of China, had been taken by the Imperial Japanese Army. The victorious soldiers engaged in widespread rape, looting, and murder, resulting in the deaths of an estimated 250,000–300,000 people. This poisonous episode, like many of Japan's wartime atrocities, remains unrecognized, unhealed, and yet to be atoned for. Such episodes – of which there are all too many – will remain stumbling blocks to reconciliation until the perpetrating nation acknowledges its guilt and offers adequate apologies and reparations.

Though Japan was busy fighting the divided but powerful Chinese, it did not loosen its grip on the Korean people. An unknown number of Korean nationals were abducted and experimented upon by the horrifying Unit 731. This unit was officially called the "Epidemic Prevention and Water Purification Department" – a tragically ironic name – and was part of a large division of the Imperial Japanese Army.

Unit 731 was in reality a covert chemical and biological warfare research unit which pioneered (in parallel with Nazi scientists) the most brutal and inhumane repertoire of experimentation ever carried out on living subjects. The test victims included resistance fighters, political prisoners, and other dissenters, including any known associates and even their families. No exceptions were made for the young, the old, or the pregnant.

The unit studied, among other things, the human body's response to extreme conditions including massive haemorrhage, induced gangrene, organ loss, extremes of heat, cold, and pressure, live vivisection, exposure to weaponized gases, and the injection of aggressive chemicals. They placed test subjects in isolation to study the process of fatal starvation; they spun victims in centrifuges until they died to understand the limits of the human body; they injected subjects with sea water, animal blood, and urine, all in the name of research.

Unit 731 bred bubonic plague-infected fleas that were "successfully" delivered via bombs onto the civilian populations in China, killing uncountable numbers of people. They even supplied infected food and chemical candles to unsuspecting civilians to study the effects.

As the Second Sino-Japanese War slid into the wider conflict of the Second World War, fresh attempts to absorb Korean culture got under way. The Japanese authorities implemented *Sōshi-kaimei*, a policy of forced name change to ensure that every Korean was given a Japanese-style family name. Within business, government, and the military, any individual with a Japanese-sounding name would progress more rapidly than anyone with a Korean-sounding one. The pressure to participate in assimilation came from all angles.

As the war progressed, Japan attempted to plug its labour gap by forced conscription of Korean workers into the Japanese-controlled mines and factories in Korea and also on mainland Japan. In Japan alone, an estimated 60,000 Korean workers died as a result of mistreatment, malnutrition, and hard labour. Many died under the onslaught of Allied bombings. Statistics for deaths under Japanese forced service in Korean and Japanese-held territories further north vary wildly from just under 300,000 to over 800,000.

Conscription into the Japanese-controlled Korean Army also intensified. The purpose of the historically titled "Chosen Army" was to repel potential Soviet incursions into Korea and to put down nationalist uprisings. As many of the northern resistance fighters and nationalists were old Korean army veterans, the encounters set Korean soldier against Korean soldier under the orders of the Japanese.

The physical enslavement of Korean people by the Japanese was not restricted to forced labour and conscription. An estimated 200,000 Korean girls and young women were sent by the occupying government to Japanese soldiers in combat as "comfort women" to boost morale. This large-scale, organized, and state-sanctioned gang rape of young Korean women has never been acknowledged by any subsequent Japanese government and no apology has been made, despite a weekly protest outside the Japanese Embassy in Seoul by surviving Korean "comfort women" since the end of the Second World War. Even today, when the surviving victims are increasingly elderly and frail, Japan's refusal to acknowledge pre-war and wartime atrocities remains a significant stumbling block to Koreans in both North and South. Korean–Japanese relations will not improve until this changes.

By 1945, the Japanese campaign in the Pacific had become desperate. The Chosen Army was reorganized into the Japanese Seventeenth Area Army and sent to face the advancing Russians. By this time, most of the veteran soldiers within the Chosen Army had already been transferred to reinforce beleaguered units around the Pacific region, leaving only reservists, conscripts, and the home guard to face the Red Army. They fled before it.

After the deployment of atomic bombs at Hiroshima and Nagasaki, Japan surrendered to the Allied forces. With Japan's defeat came the official end of the occupation, but Korea was still not free from foreign forces. As Soviet armour rolled south into Korea, stopping at the 38th Parallel, American troops landed at Incheon, west of Seoul, and marched north to meet them.

CHAPTER 3

Communism and the North

On 15 April 1912, Kim Song-ju was born in Manchuria, beyond Korea's northern border, to exiled Korean nationalists. His parents were committed Presbyterian Christians, having come from families of ministers and pastors, and they raised their boy within the church. His mother was well known and active in her church community and his father underwent education at the Sungsil Academy, an exclusive and highly competitive Christian school run by American missionaries, where each pupil was required to undertake a minimum of five hours of Bible study every week in addition to the comprehensive curriculum of subjects.

Years later, after Kim Song-ju had adopted the name "Kim Il-sung" and set his propagandists to rewriting his own past, he claimed that his father had "strenuously fought against [the] American missionary gangs who were the managers of the school, as well as the school authorities, demanding a reduction in the number of hours for religious study and an increase in those of natural sciences…".

There is no evidence to back up this claim. Though Kim Il-sung's father did in fact leave school early to join the *Chosun Kungminhoe* (Korean National Association, or KNA), it was at a time of intense national crisis and does not imply any disagreement with the school management. The DPRK biography also falsely claims that Kim Il-sung's father founded the KNA, rather than simply joining it as an ordinary member. By the time Kim Il-sung's father actually joined the KNA, it had become engaged in anti-Japanese activities and was disbanded by the Japanese police within the year.

Kim Il-sung spent almost all of his childhood away from Korea, in Manchuria, except for only two school years between the ages of 11 and 12. In 1926, when Kim Il-sung was only 14, his father died. A year later, he was detained for taking part in a play criticizing Japanese rule. In 1929, he was arrested and imprisoned for seven months for attending a Communist youth group. After his release, he was banned from returning to school altogether.

By 1931 Japan had completed the annexation of Manchuria, gaining total control of the region. In an effort to claim legitimacy for their actions, the Japanese invented the state of "Manchukuo" and installed Henry Pu Yi, a descendant of the Manchu emperors, on the throne. The Japanese and their Manchukuo puppets were fiercely resisted by Chinese communists and nationalists alike, with significant help from Korean exiles. Nevertheless, the Chinese fighters treated their Korean allies with disdain and often cruelty. Chinese commanders preferred to send Korean guerrillas on dangerous and often unnecessarily suicidal missions rather than risk their own troops. Likewise, they would plunder ethnically Korean villages as mercilessly as did the Japanese.

Kim Il-sung joined the Communist guerrillas and proved to be an effective leader. By 1932 he was leading over a dozen men, predominantly ethnic Koreans, and carrying out raids against the Japanese forces. By 1936 Kim Il-sung was commanding 100 men and had a price on his head of 20,000 yen. Guerrilla units such as his were generally poorly armed, often engaging Japanese tanks with improvised weaponry, which required some degree of bravery. This made him necessarily resourceful, because neither the Russian nor the Chinese Communists would trust the Korean exiles enough to send them arms or equipment. The gap was often filled by brutality, ruthless criminality, extortion, kidnapping, and protection scams. When ransoms went unpaid, the guerrillas took whatever steps were necessary to have their demands met. There are accounts of victims having their ears cut off and, if no ransom payment was forthcoming, they murdered them. Ethnic Koreans were not exempt from such terror tactics and the Korean fighters did not discriminate between their victims.

Having grown up in Chinese territory and being fluent in Mandarin, Kim Il-sung was better placed than most guerrilla leaders to get on within the Chinese military hierarchy. While the North-East Anti-Japanese United Army of Chinese Communists was being torn to shreds by the Japanese war machine, Kim Il-sung rose through the ranks at an impressive rate. By 1940 he was commanding 300 men, a considerable force in guerrilla warfare, and the price on his head was 200,000 yen – equal to the reward for Yang Jingyu, Commander of the First Route Army of the larger North-East Anti-Japanese Army.

His meteoric rise was aided by the deaths in combat of his fellow officers and even by defections among his own commanders. Resistance to the Japanese was crumbling at an alarming rate. His men were deserting and even the more loyal among Kim Il-sung's closest supporters turned against him in an effort to escape the conflict and win the massive bounty on their leader's head. His growing paranoia, in many ways well founded, led him to summarily execute his own officers and men at the slightest sign of perceived disloyalty.

By the winter of 1940, with both the hated Japanese and his own men gunning for him, Kim Il-sung escaped to the USSR, taking his pregnant wife with him. They spent the next four years in a Soviet training camp, bringing up their son, Kim Jong-il, who was born on 16 February 1941. Though he spent the last few years of the war away from combat, Kim Song-ju (as he was still called) had heard the name of a legendary resistance fighter from the north of Korea – Kim Il-sung. The name meant "becoming the sun", and this mysterious figure was surrounded by stories of heroic resistance to the Japanese. On 19 September 1945, Kim Song-ju boarded a Russian boat bound for Korea and, when it docked, a resistance fighter calling himself Kim Il-sung stepped off onto the peninsula. Kim Song-ju was gone for good and, so it seemed, a living legend had arrived in Korea.

The country was in utter chaos. The south in particular lacked any kind of infrastructure. The retreating Japanese had destroyed roads, railways, power stations, and factories as they went. Korea was without basic services, transport, and methods of communication, and the danger of a power vacuum threatened. In an effort to fill it, the Soviet and American representatives agreed, in principle, to enable the formation of a trustee government that would hand over power to the Korean people within five years.

The two strongest indigenous factions vying to form a domestic government in Korea were the Communists and the nationalist Korean government-in-exile that had been elected in Shanghai in 1920 under Dr Syngman Rhee. As president of the government-in-exile, Syngman Rhee was the popular choice for many, having been both a long-standing symbol of Korean nationalism in the dark years of the occupation and an outspoken critic of Japanese conduct. Other, less prominent, nationalist groups existed, but could not match their fellow nationalist's proven credentials. Many of these groups settled for working with Syngman Rhee against the shared threat posed by the Communists.

The Communist faction was split into three rival subgroups: the domestic Communists, who had endured the occupation in Korea; the Yenan Communists, who had fought in China with Mao Zedong against the Japanese; and the Soviet Communists, who had waged their campaign against the Japanese forces in Russian territories. Kim Il-sung and his supporters were among the third group so, naturally, the occupying Soviet forces favoured Kim Il-sung's party and put pressure on the opposing groups, even disarming a large group of Yenan Communists trying to re-enter their own country.

For Kim Il-sung to rise to party and country leadership, the powerful domestic faction had to be dealt with. This happened with relative ease. At the Second Congress of the Korean Workers Party (KWP), the Soviet Communists accused their rivals of collaboration. It was a charge they themselves could easily avoid, having lived outside Japanese rule. Even for those domestic Communists who had stood firm and endured the persecution of the Japanese without the least hint of collaboration, the same tactic of character assassination proved equally effective. They were simply accused of individualism and glory-seeking at the expense of the Party and, unbelievably, they were successfully discredited. Few were returned to office and the path was made clear for Kim Il-sung to become Vice-Chairman of the KWP.

In April 1946 Kim Il-sung strengthened his power by paying court to Stalin in Moscow. The visit was highly successful for the KWP's new Vice-Chairman. Having pledged tens of thousands of Korean workers for Soviet labour camps, he returned to Korea with his bid for power ratified by the world's second superpower. When Chairman Kim Tu-bong moved to another position of power, Kim Il-sung had no significant obstacle left between himself and the chairmanship of the KWP.

Though the Japanese forces had long withdrawn, the effects of their policies of suppression and societal demolition could still be felt. There were simply not enough individuals sufficiently trained in governance and management to get the country moving. Korea was administratively crippled. In the North, positions of power were filled by members of Kim Il-sung's circle, supported by other members of the Soviet Communist faction. In the south, American personnel were put in positions of authority over Koreans to help fill the void – the result was outrage and indignation. Yet again, it seemed to the Korean people, more foreigners were in power in Korea.

The Communists seized the opportunity to gain political ground by appealing to the ingrained isolationism of the Korean people, inflamed as it was by their recent suffering at the hands of external powers. They launched the General Ideological Mobilization Campaign for Nation-Building, which, as later described by Kim Jong-il, was a campaign to "do away with the survivals of Japanese imperial ideals and feudal ideas and to arm people with the idea of nation-building".[10] Though it was supposed to be a campaign for the "Koreanization" of society and a purge of everything deemed foreign, it was, in practice, a tool to break up non-governmental powers including the local "people's committees" and churches in the name of patriotism. More Korean blood was spilled as the Soviet forces aided the effort to eliminate religion in northern Korea by arresting and executing priests and missionaries.

The result was a massive internal displacement of people. The vast majority of the migrants were refugees fleeing southwards to safety. A smaller number of people moved from the south to the north; these were southern Communists, each seeking a place in the emerging Communist government. As the USA and USSR met to discuss the reunification of Korea as a single nation, the two states on the peninsula polarized.

A second round of international talks, held in May 1947, failed to reach an agreement. Later that year, in September, the USA passed a resolution at the UN Security Council that free elections should be held to appoint a home government. The USSR lost its chance to veto the motion because the

---

10. "Giving priority to ideological work is essential", Kim Jong-il, 19 June 1995.

Soviet representatives were absent, boycotting the UN entirely; nevertheless, it was patently clear that Russia would ensure elections were not allowed in the north.

In May 1948, elections to a National Assembly were held in the south and, following the creation of a Korean Constitution in July, Dr Syngman Rhee was elected president of the Republic of Korea (ROK).[11] The Communists in the north responded by electing Kim Il-sung prime minister of the Supreme People's Assembly, with a constitution very similar to that of the USSR. Stalin's government rushed to recognize the legitimacy of the Democratic People's Republic of Korea (DPRK) in the north, just as the USA moved quickly to recognize the Republic of Korea (ROK) in the south. Interested states within the international community acknowledged whichever of the two Korean republics was closest to their own political ideology. Naturally, the Communist bloc states stood behind the DPRK and the likes of Great Britain, France, and the still-nationalist China sided with the southern ROK. Neither Korean government recognized or even acknowledged the existence of the other.

As the northern infrastructure had survived better under Japanese ravages, Kim Il-sung's North Korea enjoyed an economic surge, supported by a massive influx of aid from Soviet Russia. Though Kim Il-sung sought and obtained economic aid from Stalin, he was unable to win the dictator's full confidence. The south was not without any advantages, however, as the population of the ROK was double that of the DPRK. This meant that there were more workers for rebuilding and a larger pool of indigenous talent from which to draw ministers, managers, and artisans.

Russia and America withdrew their troops and, by June 1949, Korea was at last free of foreign troops. Though an obvious

---

11. Since known as the First Republic of South Korea.

PR victory for both the ROK and the DPRK governments, this was not good news for the northern Communists. The USSR had trained and equipped the DPRK army, turning them from ragged partisans into a formidable force, but Kim Il-sung lost the close support of his most powerful allies when the Soviet troops pulled out.

The existence of the southern state remained a direct threat to the north as well as a prize to be won. Kim Il-sung urged Stalin to support him in a war against the south, but he refused. The USSR did not yet have nuclear weapons in its arsenal and could not risk local strife escalating into a wider conflict or even a third world war. Kim Il-sung would have to wait until Stalin could truly match the firepower of the US. In the south, Syngman Rhee was also appealing for supplies and support in another peninsula war. Though co-operative on many issues, the US could not risk a larger conflict and refused the ROK president's requests for arms and armour. The two states could do nothing except dig in along the 38th Parallel.

Kim Il-sung focused on consolidating his power within the borders of North Korea. He took revenge for the perceived electoral slight he'd received from Korean Presbyterians who had not voted for him in the earlier "elections". He conducted a purge of churches and clergy, and waged a war of intimidation and assassination against his opponents of all kinds. He also established the Kandong Political Institute under the popular southern defector Pak Hon-yong. Pak had express orders to train North Korean agents for infiltration and insurgency against the south, and he maintained that as many as 200,000 Koreans could rise up in the south against the ROK government.

The Institute was largely a failure, as the ROK police succeeded in arresting thousands of northern agents. But this did not prevent Pak Hon-yong from gaining political advancement; he was appointed Deputy Prime Minister and Foreign Minister of the DPRK in September 1948, and became an outspoken advocate of total war with the south.

On 29 August 1949, the successful test of the USSR's RDS-1 "First Lightning" nuclear device changed everything for Kim Il-sung and the DPRK warmongers. This 22-kiloton bomb was marginally more powerful than the "Fat Man" atomic bomb which had devastated Nagasaki almost exactly four years earlier, on 9 August 1945. The USSR's possession of such technology signalled a new phase in the Cold War and shook the notion of American supremacy, causing the panicking US to redouble its efforts to build a hydrogen bomb.

By 1950 Stalin was in a position to match America's city-destroying capabilities and felt confident that a peninsula war could therefore be limited to a local conflict. The USSR would provide the DPRK with materials and further military training in exchange for a short, sharp war which would unify Korea under Communism and destroy the American-sponsored southern government for good. Kim Il-sung insisted that DPRK forces would overrun the south within three months. Stalin agreed to support the war.

Though Kim Il-sung's life experience had taught him to trust the Soviet Communists over the Chinese and Yenan Communists, he still thought it prudent to seek Communist China's support for another conflict. Mao Zedong, now in power and seeking to strengthen Communism in the Asiatic region, was receptive to his neighbour's solicitation and agreed to provide what the Soviets would not – massed battalions of combat-ready troops.

North Korea was ready for war.

CHAPTER 4

The Korean War

On 25 June 1950, in retaliation for an invented South Korean raid, the Korean People's Army of the DPRK crossed the 38th Parallel behind a barrage of artillery fire. They claimed that Syngman Rhee and the ROK army had invaded first, and the DPRK action was to bring justice by arresting the President of the Republic of Korea and executing him. The better-trained, better-equipped, and combat-hardened KPA veterans overwhelmed the hitherto-untested ROK army. With superior firepower and 100,000 more soldiers than their southern cousins, the North Korean army quickly took ground, forcing President Rhee to evacuate his cabinet from Seoul on 27 June 1950. Seoul fell the next day.

Brutality ensued on both sides. Syngman Rhee ordered what is known as the Bodo League Massacre,[12] which began on 28 June 1950. It was a war crime in which an unknown number of southern Communists, their alleged sympathizers, and other political prisoners were murdered and buried in mass graves. Estimates of the numbers killed vary from 100,000 to as high as 1,200,000. On the same day, North Korean soldiers entered Seoul and annihilated a ROK platoon guarding the city's National University Hospital. A bloodbath ensued inside the hospital, in which the DPRK soldiers went from ward to ward, killing 900 unarmed civilians, patients, wounded soldiers, and medical personnel.

---

12. The Bodo League was a name for the National Rehabilitation and Guidance League, Syngman Rhee's 1949 "re-education" programme, designed to identify, imprison, and reform Communists. Rhee widened the programme to include dissenters and political opponents of all stripes.

The UN Security Council condemned the DPRK's invasion of the south and passed Resolution 82 demanding the north's immediate withdrawal. Resolution 83 quickly followed, enabling UN member states to lend armed assistance to South Korea. US President Harry S. Truman immediately authorized air and sea support for South Korea. The Russian representatives were still boycotting the UN and believed that the Security Council could not act without them. They claimed the international intervention was illegal, but they could not stop it. Had they been present, they might have argued that the outbreak of fighting was a civil conflict and beyond the remit of the United Nations.

Even with help from the Eighth United States Army, the southern forces could not contain the advance of the DPRK's Korean People's Army. Defeat after defeat followed the Americans' first encounter with northern forces, in which Task Force Smith, comprising 400 soldiers from the US 24th Infantry Division, attacked DPRK tanks with insufficient weaponry. Their M9 launchers fired salt-eroded rockets left over from the Second World War, which failed to detonate and simply bounced off the tanks' modern armour. Unsurprisingly, the US force was taken apart by the advancing column and the South Korean and UN coalition troops were pushed back all the way from Osan, near Seoul, to the port city of Pusan on the far south-eastern tip of the Korean peninsula.

UN and South Korean forces established a 225-kilometre-long perimeter along the Naktong River and held it against repeated assaults from northern forces. Though the DPRK army sustained heavy casualties, they did not let up the pressure on the south and made frequent assaults up and down the line. Of the 90,000 northern soldiers and hundreds of T-34 tanks, the DPRK army lost almost 60,000 men and a significant proportion of their tanks, and were forced to supplement their numbers through conscription and by bringing down less experienced and less well trained troops from other divisions.

Kim Il-sung had promised his Chinese and Soviet allies a swift victory but, although the initial conflict had gone well, China did not share his confidence. Zhou Enlai, China's first premier serving under Mao Zedong, secured Soviet air cover[13] for the 260,000 Chinese troops that he stationed along the North Korean border as a contingency against the war's escalation.

For the time being the UN forces held the skies. The DPRK's problems worsened as the US Air Force conducted sortie after sortie, destroying roads, troop columns, supply depots, and the remaining bridges. This meant that the DPRK army supply route was significantly disrupted, limiting their options and slowing their momentum. More troops and tanks arrived from US bases in Japan and by September 1950 the UN forces were ready to deliver a powerful counter-attack and punch through the Pusan Perimeter.

The primary counter-attack was not, however, to be made by crossing the Naktong River. The First Marine Provisional Brigade, who had played a central role in the perimeter's defence, were pulled back to the port at Pusan, where they boarded ship and joined a fleet carrying the US Tenth Corps from Japan. Their mission was to sail around Korea to Incheon, near Seoul, and spearhead Operation Chromite, an amphibious assault on the port's unsuspecting North Korean defenders.

Incheon was near the strategic and symbolic prize of Seoul, and sufficiently far north on the peninsula to disembowel the DPRK army's campaign in the south. The plan was

---

13. In a tragic twist of diplomatic and operational irony, the Russian Mikoyan-Gurevich (MiG)-15 fighter jets were powered by British-designed Rolls Royce Nene engines, supplied to the USSR in an earlier gesture of diplomatic goodwill by the Labour government of the time. It was these advanced MiG jets that so effectively knocked the American F-80 Shooting Stars out of the air over Korea.

masterminded by veteran army general Douglas MacArthur, who had been unanimously appointed as Commander-in-Chief of the United Nations Command. MacArthur was not without critics, however, as many of his fellow generals did not share his confidence that the planned amphibious assault would work.

Operation Chromite was anything but a simple beach landing. The plan involved infiltration and intelligence-gathering by Korean agents, a sustained naval bombardment, multiple beach landings under fire, the capture of a lighthouse, and a risky approach up two narrow and easily mined passages to a small harbour with high sea walls. The North Korean defenders had the benefit of natural and artificial defences and, thanks to Chinese intelligence, knew that an assault was likely.

Had such a risky operation failed, MacArthur would have been universally criticized as an incompetent has-been who threw away his soldiers' lives on a suicidal assault. Thankfully for him and the thousands of men storming the beaches and sea walls, the DPRK forces collapsed under the massive seaborne bombardment and the port was taken with very few UN casualties. The five-day operation, which began on 15 September and ended on 19 September, was an absolute success. The gamble paid off and MacArthur was quickly hailed as a strategic genius and a brilliant tactical commander.

Meanwhile the US Eighth Army broke out of the Pusan Perimeter and chased the collapsing DPRK army north. Because MacArthur's primary objective after Incheon was the capture of Seoul and not the immediate obliteration of the DPRK army, US forces in the north did not block their path and an estimated 30,000 enemy soldiers escaped from the rout at Pusan back across the 38th Parallel.

On 1 October 1950, the UN and US forces pushed north across the border between the warring Korean states, quickly followed by the southern ROK army. Kim Il-sung sent desperate requests to his Chinese and Soviet allies, and Stalin requested that Mao Zedong move his forces into North Korea. Mao Zedong ordered three divisions of the People's Volunteer Army of China to begin a brilliant series of 19 night marches across Manchuria and into North Korea.

By marching between 7 p.m. and 3 a.m., and ensuring they were hidden between 5 a.m. and 7 p.m., a vast number of Chinese soldiers evaded US airborne reconnaissance throughout a 286-mile march into North Korean territory. Chinese commanders were under orders to shoot any soldier breaking from their hiding places outside the hours of darkness. Though US intelligence was aware of Chinese activity along the border, they were not aware that 270,000 enemy troops were preparing to enter the combat zone.

By 19 October, the northern capital city of Pyongyang was in MacArthur's hands, along with 135,000 DPRK prisoners of war. On the same day, the Chinese forces crossed the Yalu River into North Korea. MacArthur believed it necessary to continue the advance into Chinese territory to destroy the supply depots that were responsible for supporting the DPRK war effort, but President Truman disagreed and ordered him to stop.

On 25 October, the Chinese forces launched a series of daring ambushes against the unprepared UN forces, using a brilliant combination of light arms and camouflage. They crushed the ROK army and then destroyed the right flank of the US Eighth Army, sending the UN forces into a hurried retreat. Instead of capitalizing on their victory, the Chinese army withdrew, vanishing into the mountains as unexpectedly as they had emerged.

MacArthur's command believed the Chinese withdrawal signalled their unwillingness to intervene further in North Korea, and the UN forces continued to pursue the remaining DPRK forces. China intervened again a month later on

25 November with very similar results: the Chinese surrounded the UN armies, capturing or killing an astonishing 11,000 soldiers in the first two days of fighting.

In the west of North Korea, the destruction of the ROK army and the defeat of the US Second Infantry Division began the longest retreat in American military history. They began an all-out retreat, abandoning Pyongyang in the rush southwards. The US Air Force had also lost the skies to the sudden apparition of the MiG-15 jets, and the US Command reeled from the shock. It was not until early December that the newly arrived F-86 Sabre fighter jets redressed the balance.

In the east, the US Tenth Corps struggled south through the mountains amid temperatures of minus 30 degrees centigrade. The reassertion of the US presence in the air brought relief to some of the 20,000 American marines fighting around the Chosin Reservoir. The most badly injured and frostbitten were evacuated by air; the majority left behind faced a gruelling march southwards, harried on all sides by six Chinese divisions and the deadly Korean weather. The Chinese soldiers also suffered terribly amid the snowstorms – fear of American air strikes prevented them from lighting fires for cooking or warmth, and a large number of the Chinese casualties in the war were from death by freezing.

On 10 December, the Tenth Corps survivors marched into the eastern port city of Hungnam. There was little will among the leadership to establish another perimeter and fight, so the men were duly evacuated. Before they left, American engineers destroyed any food, supplies, equipment, and infrastructure that could be of use to the Chinese, without any regard for the civilian population. People fought in the streets for the remaining food. As the US warships left, they bombarded Hungnam, inflicting yet more death and grief on the city and leaving the survivors with nowhere to go and nothing to live on.

The UN forces were in a state of panic. America feared the domino effect in which small nation after nation would fall to Communist coups and threaten Western freedom. President Truman considered the use of a nuclear response to the Korean crisis in the event of Communist domination under Kim Il-sung and his Chinese and Soviet sponsors.

"If the United Nations yields to the forces of aggression, no nation will be safe or secure," he said in a news conference on 30 November 1950. "If aggression is successful in Korea, we can expect it to spread throughout Asia and Europe to this hemisphere. We are fighting in Korea for our own national security and survival... This new act of aggression in Korea is only a part of a worldwide pattern of danger to all the free nations of the world."

On 16 December 1950 Truman declared a national state of emergency in America and initiated the mass rearmament of US forces worldwide.

There were more disasters to come. On 23 December 1950 General Walton Walker, commander of the US Eighth Army, was killed in a road accident. His replacement, Lieutenant-General Matthew Ridgway, had been in post for only five days when the Chinese People's Volunteer Army launched a bewildering attack on UN forces on 31 December, allowing the DPRK army to take Seoul again on 4 January 1951. As part of their tactics, the Chinese army banged loud gongs and blew trumpets to disorientate their enemies and to transmit tactical orders within the music, unintelligible to the UN troops on the ground. The result was utter confusion, and many American, international, and ROK troops abandoned their posts in panic.

It was not all bad news, however. Within weeks, the charismatic General Ridgway began to reverse the course of the war. His leadership style reassured his demoralized men, and they began to think and act with positivity. His change in tactics greatly boosted their confidence. There were no more rushed advances in which men and equipment were surrounded and swallowed by enemy forces. Instead, any advance was carried out at full strength, comprehensively supported by air, armour, and artillery. His troops came to call it the "meat grinder".

Success came quickly and the US troops took Seoul again on 14 March 1951. It was the city's fourth conquest in less than nine months and the place was almost unrecognizable. The population had shrunk from 1.5 million to 200,000 and lacked any kind of amenity and all basic supplies. Food was scarce and families scavenged amid the rubble. Ridgway pushed further north, meeting success by grinding down enemy resistance with long-range bombardment.

On 11 April 1951 President Truman relieved General MacArthur of his command. MacArthur had become increasingly insubordinate and was considered disrespectful of presidential authority. He returned to the US to face congressional hearings in May and June, which found that he had defied the orders of the President, the Commander-in-Chief, and had drawn the international community into a costly war when he ordered the first advance across the 38th Parallel.

Truman appointed Ridgway as Supreme Commander in Korea, who responded by pushing the Chinese and DPRK forces back up north beyond the 38th Parallel. His advance stalled when China counter-attacked with 700,000 men and by 10 July 1951 a stalemate had been reached in the fighting. Protracted armistice negotiations began and, for two years, the fighting continued alongside the talks with little gain on either side.

The talks – between North and South and their powerful backers – began at Kaesŏng in North Korea before relocating to Panmunjom, on the border shared by North and South Korea. One of the most significant stumbling blocks was the repatriation of prisoners of war. Too many of the captured

DPRK and Chinese soldiers refused to be repatriated to the north and the UN was unwilling to send them, which greatly displeased Kim Il-sung and his Chinese allies. The Neutral Nations Repatriation Commission was established to deal with the problem.

At length an armistice agreement was signed, on 27 July 1953. The Korean Demilitarized Zone (DMZ) was defined where the fighting finished, roughly along the 38th Parallel, and both North Korea and South Korea fortified their sides against further assault. Kim Il-sung returned to office with the signing of the armistice and set about building a workers' paradise from the bloody ruins of his own war.

Kim Il-sung in the Korean War

Beyond the obvious and tragic exception of starting the Korean War by invading the south, Kim Il-sung played a relatively minor role in the waging of it. Initially buoyed up by heavy armour and superiority in numbers in the rush to Pusan, Kim Il-sung enjoyed success as the DPRK's leader in the war. However, once met by a reinforced and reinvigorated US army, his success vanished as he was outmanoeuvred and outgunned until his forces were pushed back to the far north of the country.

It might have been different. Kim Il-sung ignored his Soviet and Chinese advisers, failing to choose between the two better strategies of reinforcing Incheon against amphibious assault or withdrawing to another defensive line at Seoul. This was to the particular chagrin of the Chinese, who had provided him with specific intelligence regarding the US-led Operation Chromite. Stalin had also sent his top general, M. V. Zakharov (who later became Marshal of the Soviet Union), to advise the DPRK leadership on strategy. In September 1950, Zakharov advised Kim Il-sung to abandon the failing Pusan Perimeter and defend Seoul with a greater concentration of well-equipped veteran troops. Kim Il-sung failed to take his advice and lost not only his best men, Pusan, and Seoul, but Stalin's confidence as well.

Once the Chinese entered the conflict, Kim Il-sung was almost completely sidelined as a war leader. As he had done in the later years of the Second World War, Kim Il-sung spent much of the Korean War out of the country, touring other Communist states, seeking support and urging further involvement by his allies.

Unsurprisingly, the North Korean regime gives a rather different account. The Korean Central News Agency, the official news network of the DPRK, reports that the "Fatherland Liberation War" was a war started by America, the "imperialist aggressor", with South Korean support. The war did not limp to a stalemate either: America was roundly defeated and driven out thanks to "the unshakable iron will and pluck, gifted military wisdom and strategy and tactics of Kim Il-sung". The DPRK's Great Leader even performed "epoch-making miracles and exploits in the struggles to defend socialism and build a rich and powerful country". China and Russia are hardly mentioned.

Since 1953, the widely accepted end to the "hot" phase of the war, the DPRK regime has maintained a warlike stance. The North Korean army remains one of the largest standing armies in the world, with over a million soldiers, and the DPRK regime regularly engages in sabre-rattling. In 1975, Kim Il-sung tried to reignite the conflict, having been inspired by the North Vietnamese army's capture of Saigon in the Vietnam War. He visited Mao Zedong to beg for military aid but was refused. In more recent times, there have been numerous breaks in the armistice, such as the sinking on 26 March 2010 of the South Korean warship *Cheonan* by a North Korean submarine and the shelling of Yeonpyeong Island in the same year.

In North Korea and in the minds of its indoctrinated people, it is as if the conflict ended only yesterday. America looms on the border, desperate to invade, and a state of war persists. Sadly, there is one shred of truth within the tangle of DPRK propaganda regarding the Korean War: the armistice did not mark the legal end of the war.

No peace treaty was ever signed and, even now, the two Koreas are still technically at war.

CHAPTER 5

The Coming of Christianity
to Korea

Koreans are generally deeply religious people – and South Korea has diverse and mutually respectful religious traditions which have played an essential role in developing the dynamic state it is today. Its democratic institutions, social structures, voluntary endeavour, and dynamic economy owe much to people of faith who fought against the oppression and injustice meted out by the Japanese and subsequent dictatorships.

In the North, the DPRK Constitution theoretically allows religious belief but, in reality, loyalty is owed only to the party and the state. In the aftermath of the Korean War religious practice was asphyxiated in the North and Christianity, in particular, was singled out and caricatured as a tool of the Americans. In reality, it was a religious belief that was primarily brought to Korea by Koreans, and one which, when Pyongyang was known as "the Jerusalem of the East", played and could once again play a significant role in providing education, health, and food, as well as spiritual values.

The story of Korean Christianity was commemorated in 1984, when Pope John Paul II visited the flat sands of the Han River in South Korea to canonize 47 Korean women, 46 Korean men, seven French priests, and three French bishops who were all martyred for their Christian faith. It was the first time that such a ceremony had been performed outside Rome. Those chosen for sainthood were representative of the many thousands who lost their lives because they refused to renounce their religious beliefs. Pope John Paul II described the Korean church as "a community unique in the history of the church".

It is not only the unimaginable suffering endured by the Korean church that makes it unique; it is also the manner in which Christianity came to the Hermit Kingdom. The church in Korea was not born from foreign missionaries converting the Korean population; it was formed by individual Koreans seeking out the gospel and bringing it back to their countrymen.

The first news of Christianity came to Korea in the seventeenth century. It entered via the trade caravan that travelled each winter from Korea to the Chinese city of Peking, where goods, gifts, and slaves were taken in tribute. The returning travellers brought news of agriculture, astronomy, and mathematics in the Chinese court, part of the early "scientific diplomacy" practised by the Society of Jesus, better known as the Jesuits.

Matteo Ricci was one of the European Jesuits working to engage the Chinese court. The Cambridge scholar Mary Laven, in her superb *Mission to China: Matteo Ricci and the Jesuit Encounter with the East*,[14] charts the late-sixteenth- and early-seventeenth-century encounters of this remarkable man with China.

Laven forensically analyses the challenges that faced Ricci and his companion, Michele Ruggieri, and details more than 2,000 conversions and the widespread dissemination of the Christian narrative by Ricci's group in the Orient.

Upon reaching China, the Europeans initially shaved their heads and dressed in the style of indigenous monks, but soon realized that by identifying with Buddhist and Taoist "idolatry" they were failing to reach the literati – the educated Confucian elite. A change of tactics was in order, so Ricci chose to dress and behave as a Confucian scholar. By doing so, he was able to engage with China's culture and leadership through science, books, and reason – *fides et ratio*.

14. Published by Faber and Faber, January 2012.

"The Chinese have a wonderful intelligence, natural and acute," he wrote, "from which, if we could teach our sciences, not only would they have great success among these eminent men, but it would also be a means of introducing them easily to our holy law and they would never forget such a benefit."

Unlike his more aggressive Portuguese and Spanish counterparts, whose presence in Macau (near Hong Kong) became a source of conflict with the Chinese authorities, Ricci's admiration for Chinese culture and his embrace of the language and customs gradually made him *persona grata* in many circles.

Ricci brought the best of Western culture to the East. He published his own world map, the Mappamondo, along with translations of Western classical scholarship; he shared knowledge of astronomy and mathematics; and he imported hitherto unknown musical instruments, such as the harpsichord, along with Venetian prisms and mechanical clocks. By doing so, Ricci gained acceptance and the forbearance of the Emperor, despite the occasional attempt to close his missions.

His legacy included astronomical instruments and installations brought by Jesuits to Beijing, which remained untouched even during China's disastrous Cultural Revolution and may be seen to this day, beautifully preserved at Beijing's Ancient Observatory. An even more enduring memory has been Ricci's admirable willingness to find ways through difficult situations and his innate respect for Oriental culture and civilization.

His reasoned approach also bore spiritual fruit: the Chinese showed a keen interest in Christianity. In his diary, Ricci wrote, "From morning to night, I am kept busy discussing the doctrines of our faith. Many desire to forsake their idols and become Christians."

Ricci brought the hugely admired *Plantin Polyglot Bible* to China – eight gilded folio volumes with printed parallel texts in Aramaic, Syriac, Hebrew, Greek, and Latin. His *True*

Meaning of the Lord of Heaven was printed and distributed widely, drawing heavily on Aquinas but also appropriating Confucian ideas to bolster the Christian cause. He brilliantly repositioned the important Chinese custom of ancestor worship by tracing everything back to "the first ancestor" – the Creator, the Lord of Heaven.

Among Ricci's seventeenth-century writings were his Catechism and a treatise *On Friendship*, which built on Confucian beliefs and expressed the persuasive notion that "to have friends coming from distant places – is that not delightful?". Ricci simultaneously introduced his readers to Cicero's assertion that "the reasons for friendship are reciprocal need and mutual help". *Amicitia perfecta* – perfect friendship – was, for Ricci, the highest of ideals. The Chinese came to value him as a true friend.

On his death, on 11 May 1610, he was uniquely accorded a burial site in Peking by the Emperor, which, according to Laven, was "an extraordinary coup, which testified to the success of nearly 30 years of careful networking and diplomacy."

In 1644, over three decades after Ricci's death, the Crown Prince of Korea returned to Seoul from Peking with five baptized Chinese eunuchs and three baptized court ladies. Christianity had come to Korea.

There are also accounts from the same period in Korean records mentioning England, France, and Catholicism. Books on Christianity became prized by young, elite Koreans and some of Christianity's radical teaching about the innate value of every person began to be discussed in a country where poverty was rife, worsened by the punishing strain of paying tribute to foreign powers. The population topped 5 million but more Koreans died of famine and epidemics in 1671 than during all of Japan's repeated raids and invasions. In the century following, people stole clothes from graves, babies were abandoned, and the starving ate the dead. Floods added more misery.

It was in this climate that a young Korean intellectual, Yi Pyok, read about Christianity from Chinese books circulating among a group of friends. In 1777 he brought his friends together to conduct further study. They met in a Buddhist monastery, happily known as The Hermitage of Heavenly Truth. They concluded that the Confucian ideals of personal goodness, reverence for ancestors, and respect for the aged sat very comfortably with the Catholic tradition of the Christian faith.

Curious Korean youths were eager to plumb the depths of this religion, impressed by a doctrine in which all were loved equally by God and by the Jesuit demands for justice for the poor and an end to slavery.

On a subsequent winter embassy to Peking, one of Yi Pyok's young associates, Yi Seung-hun, travelled to China with his father and sought out the Christian community. He was baptized by a Jesuit and took the name Peter, returning to Korea in 1785. Within a year, a secret church had been established in Pyongyang. The authorities raided the house church and discovered a prayer group. The owner of the house, Thomas Kim, was so badly injured during interrogation that he died of his injuries.

That same year, 1786, belief in Christ was banned. Christianity was perceived by the most powerful of the isolationist Koreans as "Western learning", and deemed treacherous and dangerous. It omitted ancestor worship and was therefore considered "opposed to human morality".

State hostility was harsh, even toward the royals and members of the nobility who had converted. In 1790 there were 4,000 believers in Korea, and, though there were executions every year, by 1800 the number of believers had risen to 10,000. One fearful Christian penned a letter to Jesuits in China appealing for military protection. The letter was intercepted and brought to Korea's dowager queen. Immediately she decreed that to hold the evil learning was high treason. Christian belief now warranted death.

Some Christians died in prison. Many others recanted their faith under duress. One, who had renounced his beliefs and then returned to the faith and given himself up, was sentenced to "25 blows of the big paddle". The beating left him insensible and he died a few hours later.

Yi Seung-hun, who had been baptized with the name Peter, denied his faith as his namesake had done before him, only to re-embrace it later. He was martyred for doing so in 1801, along with two royal princesses, among a group of 300 Christians.

Many of the ordeals faced by prisoners are described in *The Martyrs of Korea* by the late Msgr Richard Rutt[15]: "a cord was passed under the thighs, crossed over the front then held taut by men on either side who applied a sawing motion that cut through the flesh like a cheese-cutter, right to the bone."[16] Prisoners were given boiled millet twice a day. Those who could not buy or acquire more food were reduced to eating the foul straw and lice. Many who had not recanted under torture cracked because of the unbearable conditions in prison.

Despite the persecutions, priests arrived in the country from time to time to preach. Most were executed and, for 35 years, the fledgling church was without a single priest, yet thousands came forward to be baptized.

In 1834, a French priest, Pierre Maubant, volunteered to go to Korea to minister to the country's Christians. Border guards along the Yalu River would not allow Europeans to enter, so Maubant waited until the river froze. In January 1836 he crossed into Korea, taking two weeks to walk to Seoul. Maubant was joined by two more priests, Jacques Chastan and Laurent Imbert, who became the first bishop of the Korean diocese. To

---

15. Published by Catholic Truth Society (1 February 2002).
16. A noted Korean scholar and one-time Anglican Bishop of Korea, Canon Rutt became a Catholic priest of the Plymouth Diocese (UK) and was given the title "Monsignor" by Pope Benedict XVI.

conceal their obviously European features, the three men wore capacious Korean mourning costumes and very wide-brimmed hats, carrying out their duties only at night. Within weeks, 2,000 Koreans had been baptized, bringing the total number of Christians in the country to 9,000.

Three years later, Maubant was decapitated for his faith. Hundreds of Korean Christians suffered the same brutal fate, including entire families of Christian converts who were put to death together.

Typical was Peter Yu, aged 13, who was tortured on 14 separate occasions. He remained defiant to the end, even picking up shreds of his own flesh and throwing them before his interrogators. He was strangled in prison in October 1839. He was among those canonized by John Paul II.

Most famous among the Korean martyrs is St Andrew Kim, born on 21 August 1821. Andrew was baptized at the age of 15 and was smuggled out of Korea by Father Maubant to receive theological training in China. The British consul in Shanghai arranged shelter for him and, in 1844, Andrew became the first Korean to be ordained as a priest. Later that year he recrossed the Yalu River and entered Korea as a missionary to his own people. By the autumn of 1846 he was on trial.

His eloquence and good manners impressed the judges, but the appearance of two French warships off the Korean coast inflamed the angry isolationist tendency within all Koreans. The French admiral worsened the crisis by sending insulting letters to the Korean king. Andrew's fate was sealed as the mood soured against all who "colluded" with foreigners. On 16 September 1846, aged just 25, Andrew was taken to the Han sands where he was stripped naked and decapitated.

"This is my last hour of life, listen to me attentively," he said just before he died. "If I have held communication with foreigners, it has been for my religion and for my God. It is for Him that I die.

My immortal life is on the point of beginning. Become Christians if you wish to be happy after death, because God has eternal chastisements in store for those who have refused to know Him."

It took eight strokes of the sword to kill Andrew Kim. According to custom, his head should have been displayed on a pole for three days, but the authorities were afraid of the public reaction. They buried Andrew immediately.

Seventeen years later, in 1863, Robert Jermain Thomas, a Welsh missionary, was working in Peking. There he met two Korean traders who told him of the 50,000 Christians in Korea and the painful conditions under which they lived. He secured funding from the Scottish Bible Society and travelled to bring Bibles to the beleaguered community.

Thomas obtained work as an interpreter on an American-armed trading ship, the *General Sherman*. As the schooner travelled around Korea, he handed out his Chinese-language Bibles and learned much about the Korean language and culture. The voyage went well until, in 1866, they reached the Taedong River, Pyongyang, where the vessel and its crew became involved in an altercation with Korean officials over Thomas's distribution of Christian tracts and Bibles. The authorities insisted that the trading vessel withdraw from their waters and the situation escalated into violence, in which the crew of the *General Sherman* fired their cannons upon civilians, killing a number of them and enraging the local population.

The Korean army responded by launching a fire ship, which struck the *General Sherman* and set it alight. Four crewmen were burned to death and the remainder were killed by gunfire after the schooner ran aground. Calling on the name of Jesus, Thomas leapt into the river with the only surviving crewman and together they made for the shore. Upon reaching it, they were set upon by angry civilians and beaten to death. A ferocious wave of anti-Christian persecution followed.

Before he died, Thomas pushed the very last one of his 500 Bibles into the hands of the man who killed him. The Korean authorities ordered every Bible and Christian tract to be destroyed, so this man took the Bible home and used its pages to wallpaper his house. At first, he was unaware of the significance of the writing on the walls of his home, but over time he began to read the fragmented pages of Scripture. His house became a meeting place for a Presbyterian congregation and Thomas's executioner was baptized.

The congregation established the Thomas Memorial Church nearby, which survived until further persecutions amid the Japanese occupation of Korea. Recently, the foundations of the Thomas Memorial Church were discovered in the grounds of the Pyongyang University of Science and Technology (PUST). Its founder and president, Dr James Kim, himself a survivor of the Korean War, believes it is "the hand of God bringing two histories together".

The aftermath of the *General Sherman* incident led to the 1882 trade treaty with America, in which a clause required toleration and protection for Christian missionaries. Evangelizing was still forbidden but missionaries were allowed to embark on educational and medical initiatives. This led to a fresh influx of Christians from abroad on humanitarian and aid missions.

Chosŏn King Gojong allowed Horace Allen, the first American missionary in Korea, to establish previously unknown Western medical facilities – initially known as The House of Extended Grace and later as The House of Universal Helpfulness – to train Koreans in Western medicine. The king also granted Methodist missionary Henry Appenzeller permission in 1885 to open the Pai Chai Hak Dang School (now University). Another Presbyterian, Horace Underwood, was allowed to create an orphanage which later became Gyeongsin High School. Mary F. Scranton, under the sponsorship of Chosŏn Queen Min, created Korea's first school for girls at Ewha Hak Dang, meaning "Pear Blossom Academy". Out of these humble missionary beginnings came Korea's foremost schools and universities, which shaped generation after generation.

Christianity also had a fundamental impact on the long-held core beliefs of Korean society. Many Koreans embraced Christian teaching, which revolutionized feudal attitudes towards women and children. For instance, the Catholic Church allowed widows to remarry, a practice not normally permitted in Korean society. In addition, Christianity prohibited concubinage and polygamy; it forbade cruelty to or desertion of wives; and Korean Christians taught parents that their children were all precious gifts from God – even girls. First-born sons were not the only children to be cherished. The arrival of missionary schools enabled girls to acquire an education as well as boys. The church also placed a prohibition on the traditional arranged child marriages.

Though socially progressive, the "external force" of Christianity threatened to bring about huge changes in Korean society, and was viewed by many in power as a dangerous threat to the stability of the country.

It took another external force to bring the church into the welcoming arms of the Korean people at large – the Japanese occupation.

CHAPTER 6

Occupation, Opposition, and the Church

Under Japanese rule, many Christians refused to worship the Japanese Emperor. This led to public martyrdom of the faithful and to ruptures within the Christian community as those who collaborated were ostracized. This in turn led to the identification of Christianity with Korean independence and increased the churches' standing with ordinary Koreans during the dark years of the occupation and beyond.

When discontent with Japanese rule erupted in the "March First Movement"[17] of 1919, Christians formed a large part of the assembled demonstrators. The "Righteous People's Armies",[18] marching for independence, were predominantly made up of Catholics. As the world slipped into the Second World War, the Japanese asphyxiation of Korean culture also threatened the survival of churches when worship at Shinto shrines became mandatory. Heavy penalties were paid by those refusing to take part in the Japanese religious rites.

At the end of Japanese occupation there was still a thriving Christian presence in Pyongyang, but the church was split between those who had collaborated with the Japanese and those who had not.

In 1945, Presbyterian ministers Yoon Ha-yong and Han Kyong-jik formed the Christian Social Democratic Party, the first opposition party in North Korea. Communists raided

17. See chapter 2.
18. See chapter 2.

a planning meeting at a church, resulting in the deaths of 23 people. Meanwhile, in Pyongyang, Communists arrested Christian leader Kim Hwa-sik, along with 40 others, as they met to create the Christian Liberal Party. Christianity was not going to be tolerated in Kim Il-sung's North Korea.

Kim Il-sung did not rely solely on brutality. Instead, he turned to his maternal uncle to help redirect Christian activism into collaboration with the Communists. Kang Lyang-uk had been among the church leaders who had told their congregations to worship at the Shinto shrines during Japanese rule. In 1946 the DPRK leadership helped him establish his pro-Communist Christian League. By 1949 any known Christians who refused to collaborate by joining the league had been jailed.

Alongside this move, a campaign to seize all religious property began targeting Christian churches and Buddhist temples alike. Christian schools and other church-run projects were shut down or disbanded. The campaign turned bloody and a number of anti-religious outrages were committed, such as the massacre at a cave at Wonsan, where 530 accused religious and political dissenters were murdered. Many of the victims were children. In October 1950, as the North Korean army retreated, a journalist visited the site and described the carnage: a mass grave of twisted bodies – all shot in the back of the neck.

Another foretaste of what awaited Christians in the new Communist state was the fate of some of the Christian clergy captured during the hostilities. One of the most vivid and harrowing accounts of these degradations was published in 1955 by survivor Father Philip Crosbie, an Australian missionary.

March Till They Die is the story of his imprisonment and forced march between 1950 and 1953 with hundreds of captured religious leaders. The title of Father Crosbie's book is drawn from the remarks of a North Korean soldier. When Salvation Army Commissioner Herbert Lord protested that the elderly or infirm among the prisoners would "die if they have to march", the Korean major responded, "Then let them march until they die."

During their epic ordeal, Father Crosbie and the column of victims were marched from place to place, given starvation rations, and frequently left exposed to the elements. Catholic priests from America and Ireland marched and died alongside senior Anglicans, Salvation Army leaders, and Methodist missionaries. There were even groups of nuns among them.

Mother Beatrix, the 76-year-old provincial superior of a group of French nuns, was forced to endure the miles and the exposure. Having given more than 50 years of her life to caring for the sick, the poor, and orphans in Korea, she fell by the roadside when she could walk no further. One of the guards shot her dead where she lay. Belgian Carmelite Mother Mechtilde received the same treatment, as did Maryknoll Bishop Patrick Byrne.

Father Crosbie recorded Bishop Byrne's hasty burial: "The only sign of his rank was a light cassock of black silk, with red buttons and piping. The buttons under their covering of red cloth were of metal. Some day they may help to identify the remains."

Reverend Charles Hunt and Father Frank Canavan died a few days later. The remaining prisoners were marched up to the Yalu River and the Chinese border, and then back down again to Pyongyang. Very few survived.

On 25 May 1953, Father Crosbie was handed over to an official of the Soviet Union, taken to Moscow, and – incredibly – freed. Staff at the Australian Embassy welcomed him: "And so", he wrote, "I came to freedom [in] a land where the Muses are not completely chained to the chariots of politicians; where books and newspapers are freely published, and I can freely read them. All this I prize; but I have gained a still greater and more precious freedom. It is the freedom to believe in God and openly profess my faith."

Philip Crosbie prized his regained freedom but he also observed that the cruelty and atrocities had not just flowed in one direction; he had seen enough to know that the South Koreans had blood on their hands too. He concluded his account with a prayer for both those who had died and those who had inflicted such suffering: "May there be none of us who will not find Him at the end!"

Life did not improve for Christians in the North once the war came to an end. Kim Il-sung's efforts to stamp out religious practice continued unabated. The Communist leader believed that Korean Christians and his American opponents were more than in league – they were one and the same. In his writings Kim Il-sung frequently criticized religion as a negative force and as unscientific, while his own *Juche* philosophy of self-reliance was presented as a far superior alternative.

In Article 14 of his 1948 Constitution, Kim Il-sung did, however, decree that "citizens of the Democratic People's Republic of Korea shall have the freedom of religious belief and of conducting religious services". By 1972 this had been modified to give people "freedom to oppose religion" (Article 54), which amounted to open season on religious adherents.

Further modification came in 1992, with Article 68 granting freedom of religious belief and the right to construct buildings for religious use and religious ceremonies. It, too, was tempered by a prohibition on any person using religion "to drag in foreign powers or to destroy the state or social order". "Social order", of course, was an umbrella term for any aspect of North Korean life that the DPRK regime could scrutinize and rigidly control.

Christianity in North Korea today

After the Japanese persecutions and six decades of DPRK repression, it is impossible to know how many Christians there are in North Korea. The regime claims that, of its 24.4 million people, the numbers of religious believers are tiny: there are 10,000 Protestants, 4,000 Catholics, 10,000 Buddhists and 40,000 Neo-Confucian Cheondoists within its borders.

A report of 2005–06 by Religious Intelligence UK suggests different numbers of believers: 3,846,000 followers of Korean Shamanism; 3,245,000 Cheondoists; 1,082,000 Buddhists; and 406,000 Christians.[19] The report also lists an additional 280,000 estimated secret Christians. None of these statistics are verifiable, least of all the number of "illicit" Christians.

Becoming an illicit Christian is a serious crime, with terrifying consequences. Some believers who have escaped from North Korea say that they had never seen a church or a Bible before leaving the country. Many of those left behind are in the numerous camps and prisons, where they are kept in horrific conditions. Fed on starvation rations and routinely deprived of sleep, they are crammed into overcrowded cells where there isn't even enough room to lie down.

As recently as 2011 there have been reports of a further campaign of persecution against Christians in North Korea. At least 20 Christians were arrested and sent to the Yodok Political Prison Camp for their faith. In several meetings, I raised this case with North Korean officials, but was told that these reports were "lies" and that the execution of Christians was "impossible".

The United Nations estimates that 400,000 people have died in the camps in the past 30 years. Ironically, many of the barbaric practices that characterize the camps were pioneered by the Japanese during their occupation of the Korean peninsula. After the Korean War, the Communist regime in the North and the military dictatorship in the South used many of the same methods to stamp out dissent.

---

19. http://web.archive.org/web/20071013201130/http://www.religiousintelligence.co.uk/country/?CountryID=37

Since being elected chairman of the British Parliamentary All-Party Group on North Korea seven years ago, I have chaired several open hearings at Westminster where we have taken evidence and heard first-hand accounts from North Koreans who have escaped from prison camps – and these have included Christians.

Yoo Sang-joon was a North Korean Christian defector who came to Westminster eight years ago. Having seen his wife and children die during the famine of the 1990s, he became an "Asian Raoul Wallenberg",[20] bravely re-entering North Korea and helping people flee across the border. This led to his arrest by the Chinese who, after international pressure, sent him to South Korea rather than repatriating him to the North as they had originally intended. China's typical policy of forced repatriation of North Korean escapees, which goes against international law, has drawn rightfully severe criticism from the UN and humanitarian organizations.

On one occasion my committee was addressed by two diminutive North Korean women who, speaking through an interpreter, recounted their experiences in North Korean prison camps. From time to time their stories were interrupted as the women wept.

Jeon Young-ok was 40. When she was a little girl her mother tried to flee to China with their family by crossing the Tumen River in the north-east of the DPRK, a location I visited in September 2012. They were caught, and her father and brother imprisoned. Her mother died of heart disease and left Jeon Young-ok and her two siblings alone. Years later, she had to undertake equally risky expeditions across the North Korean border to find money and food for her children, who were

20. Raoul Wallenberg was a Swedish diplomat who rescued many tens of thousands of Jews in Nazi-occupied Hungary during the Holocaust. He used his diplomatic powers to issue Jews with passports and shelter them within the embassy building in Budapest.

suffering in the deadly famine of the 1990s. She was caught and jailed twice in her efforts to feed her family.

Movingly, she told the parliamentary hearing: "I couldn't bear to die with my children in my arms. As long as I was alive I couldn't just watch them die." Hers is just one of an uncountable number of similar stories. Many other desperate parents and their families were among the 2 million who starved to death during the famine.

Mrs Jeon was caught by Chinese authorities in 1997 and again in 2001, when she was sent back to Northern Pyeong-an Detention Camp in North Korea.

"I was put in a camp where I saw and experienced unimaginable things. We were made to pull the beards from the faces of elderly people. Prison guards treated them like animals. The women were forced to strip. A group of us were thrown just one blanket and we were forced to pull it from one another as we tried to hide our shame. I felt like an animal, no better than a pig. I didn't want to live."

Jeon Young-ok added: "They tortured the Christians the most. They were denied food and sleep. They were forced to stick out their tongue and iron was pushed into it."

Despite all this, she harbours no hatred for her country and shows extraordinary composure: "The past is not important but these terrible things are still happening in North Korea. These camps should be abolished for ever."

The story of Christianity on the Korean peninsula seems to be the perfect proof of Tertullian's ancient assertion that "the blood of martyrs is the seed of the church".[21] The shedding of so many lives did not deter Koreans from embracing Christianity. As St Augustine Yu, who was martyred along with his wife, son, and brother, said: "Once having known God, I cannot possibly betray him."

---

21. Tertullian, *Apologeticus*, chapter 50.

Wonderfully, the Christian legacy in both North and South Korea has been more than just bloody persecution and death. In the South, Christianity became the recurring theme within South Korea's social and political policy-making, thanks to the political activism of many thousands of Christians. The church even became a haven for dissenters during General Park's repressive campaigns.

During Park's time in power, a form of Christian theology emerged called Minjung. The word "Minjung" was formed from the Chinese characters *min*, which means "people", and *jung*, meaning "the mass". When combined, the phrase translates as "the common people". Minjung theology interprets the Bible, history, and the political challenges of the moment in direct relation to the lives of the common people, not the rulers or the economic elite. It is a Christian theology that puts the poor first.

Because it emphasizes justice, mercy, and compassion for the common people, Minjung is often compared with the Liberation Theology of Latin America – but with fewer Marxist connotations – and this goes some way towards explaining the easy alliance between the church and the popular democratic movements throughout Korea in the twentieth century. It was the motivating power behind several socially progressive initiatives during Park's reign, including the Catholic Farmers Movement and the Protestant Urban Industrial Mission, which campaigned for better remuneration and working conditions for agricultural and industrial workers.

Minjung also became a key influence on two Christian men who endured prison sentences for their democratic beliefs and who would be future presidents of the Republic of Korea: Presbyterian Kim Young-sam and Catholic Kim Dae-jung.

Even in the North, the story is not only of death and despair for Christians. Despite the decades of anti-Christian activity by the DPRK regime, four churches are allowed to exist in Pyongyang.

These are, of course, closely controlled by the state and overseen by the DPRK's tame "church", the Korean Christian Federation. I have spoken to the congregation at the Changchung Catholic Church and met members of the congregations at the other churches. At Changchung I met Jang Jae-on, the Communist Party official who regulates religious belief.

The meetings have shown that these churches exist to create an illusion of religious freedom. Meaningful dialogue with them is almost impossible, because their role is to control and not to enable. Nevertheless, Christian organizations have been able to get through the closed border and bring food and medicine into the country. In another conciliatory move the North Koreans have also extended an official invitation to Dr Rowan Williams, formerly the Archbishop of Canterbury, to visit the country.

Another development has been the visit of some South Korean Protestant pastors to the North. They have been permitted to hold regulated services in their churches, carry out extensive refurbishment, and build a small seminary. The students pursue a five-year course and are then admitted to the Korean Christian Fellowship as pastors upon graduation.

It was even reported that five North Koreans have been selected by Cardinal Nicholas Cheong Jin-suk to study for ordination at Seoul's Incheon University in South Korea. This would represent a highly significant step forward if they are permitted to return to the North once ordained.

Such an event was "an unfulfilled dream" of the widely admired and revered late Cardinal Stephen Kim Sou-hwan – the great champion of Korean freedom and democracy. It is an aspiration that, during each of our visits, Baroness Caroline Cox and I have repeatedly raised with the officials who control religious belief.

I allowed myself a wry smile as I arrived for my third visit to North Korea with Lady Cox in 2010 when, aboard an Air

China plane, the piped music accompanying our landing was Isaac Watts' Christmas hymn "Joy to the world! The Lord has come! Let earth receive her King". Along with the sight of diplomats from the once Marxist Russia arriving to worship at Pyongyang's Russian Orthodox church, I couldn't help but reflect on the twists and turns in ideological and social history. Though Marx was wrong in suggesting that religion is "the opium of the people", perhaps the rest of that much-cited quotation does have great application and resonance in the story of Korea, where "religion is the sigh of the oppressed creature, the heart of a heartless world, and the soul of the soulless condition".

CHAPTER 7

Post-war South: Dictatorship and Death

In the blood-soaked aftermath of the Korean War, the internationally enforced Demilitarized Zone (DMZ) brought a measure of security to South Korea but did not guarantee internal peace or prosperity. The once-exiled President Syngman Rhee, who had won his last election in 1952 partly through intimidation and imprisonment of his opponents, returned to office at the end of the war. He was re-elected for a third time in 1956 in what should have been his last presidency, but Rhee, responsible for over a million deaths in a number of bloody political purges, was unwilling to relinquish power. Soon after re-election, he forced through a constitutional amendment to remove the three-term limit on the length of time a president could hold office. The way was clear for him to "serve" an unlimited number of terms.

His governance was incompetent and corrupt. The economy stagnated and the pace of reconstruction was painfully slow. A third-world level of poverty persisted throughout his presidency and the South Korean people remained dependent on foreign aid to survive.

In 1960, Rhee ran for office for the fourth time at the age of 84. When his presidential rival, Cho Byeong-ok, died just days before the election, Rhee faced no opposition and was elected to office with a landslide 90 per cent of the vote. When Rhee's preferred vice-presidential candidate Lee Gibung was elected in another impressive and equally unrealistic landslide, the opposing Democratic Party decried the election as fixed.

On 15 March 1960, approximately 1,000 people met at the Democratic Party Headquarters in the city of Masan to protest against Rhee's political corruption. The demonstration was brutally suppressed by police, and a number of students were killed. Rhee blamed the violent disturbance on Communist insurgents from the North. By April, anger against Rhee had mushroomed. On 19 April, students from Korea University in Seoul marched on the Blue House – the presidential residence and office built on second Chosŏn-era rose gardens. As they marched, their numbers grew, and by the time they arrived they outnumbered the massed police facing them.

Rhee ordered his armed police to fire on the crowd, and over 200 students were killed and many more wounded. Despite the deaths, the "April 19 Movement" gained momentum and another march was held on 25 April, with the protesters assembling in even greater numbers. This time the police refused to fire on the demonstration, robbing Rhee of his principal weapon of suppression, as the ROK army had stayed neutral throughout the demonstrations. The next day, 26 April, Rhee was forced to resign. On 28 April Syngman Rhee and his family were rushed out of the country on a CIA-operated DC-4 airliner, heading for permanent exile in Hawaii.

By removing Rhee, the April Revolution had dismantled the First Republic of South Korea in the hope of establishing a more competent and productive government. Instead, the Second Republic of South Korea proved to be an insecure and bureaucratic administration drawn from the opposition party democrats under the new prime minister, Chang Myon. Because of Syngman Rhee's numerous abuses, the role of president was reduced almost to a ceremonial one; now it was filled by President Yun Bo-seon. Neither Prime Minister Chang nor President Yun commanded the respect or loyalty of the Democratic Party, nor could they agree on matters of policy.

As they reshuffled their cabinet again and again, dissatisfied Korean citizens and students filled the streets calling for wide-ranging political reform. Riots broke out. The discredited police could not maintain order and – to the relief of the disillusioned and exhausted public – Major-General Park Chung-hee seized power on 16 May 1961 in a military coup. The short-lived Second Republic of South Korea had already failed.

Prime Minister Chang Myon was immediately deposed but puppet-President Yun was kept in power by Park's military council to bring an air of legitimacy and continuity to the new regime. The President even proved useful to the new military junta by persuading the lingering US Eighth Army and the remaining ROK army units to keep out of this new transition in power.

At first, General Park Chung-hee and his military leadership promised to return South Korea to democratic rule at the earliest possible opportunity. On 2 December 1962 Park held a referendum on establishing a presidential system for rule, which returned an emphatic "yes" vote. Though he and his fellow generals had promised not to run in the coming presidential elections, Park ran for and won the presidency by a narrow margin over his democrat rival. By 1963, the Third Republic of South Korea had arrived.

The first decade of General Park's rule was one in which South Korea enjoyed economic growth and sovereign security unimaginable at any point in the previous 100 years. To begin with, North Korea was the larger power in both economy and industrial–military might; by the end of the 1960s, the tables had turned.

Park oversaw a programme of economic reform based on a five-year plan which supported the textile industry, promoted self-sufficiency, and redistributed international aid among South Korean businesses in the form of grants and highly favourable loans. Park also resisted the isolationist urge within Korean society. South Korea's export market ballooned as Park improved the diplomatic relationship with Japan. Though a highly controversial move, a more open diplomatic stance towards Korea's most hated historical enemy opened up new markets, and trade flourished. Park did not hesitate to crush the inevitable public backlash.[22]

General Park also sought to establish the international reputation of South Korea as a military force. In November 1961 he offered the support of South Korean troops to US President John F. Kennedy in the Vietnam War, but Kennedy refused. In May 1964, President Lyndon Johnson requested South Korean help and the first of 320,000 South Korean troops arrived later that year. The largest number of South Korean troops in Vietnam at any one time was 50,000 because none of Park's troops stayed beyond one year's tour of duty. With only 5,000 deaths among such a large deployment of men, Park gained a vast number of veteran troops and the thanks of the United States government. In addition, the USA paid $236 million for the services of the South Korean soldiers.

Not all of Park's reforms and initiatives were so beneficial. In 1961 he authorized politician Kim Jong-pil to create the Korean Central Intelligence Agency (KCIA), with orders to infiltrate opposition and quash dissent. The KCIA began by disrupting the widespread student protests and tracking the activities of South Korean citizens abroad. The KCIA constantly stretched and overreached its remit, creating a climate of fear through the unchecked detention and torture of students, political activists, and journalists.

---

22. Park even attempted to open meaningful dialogue with his North Korean neighbours, going as far as to send his intelligence chief Lee Hu-rak to meet Kim Il-sung in Pyongyang. The meeting, in May 1972, seemed to go well but all dialogue was severed two years later after the second of two assassination attempts by North Korean agents against Park.

The KCIA even engaged in the kidnap of South Korean nationals abroad. The most high-profile kidnapping came in August 1973 in Tokyo, when the KCIA abducted Kim Dae-jung, the Catholic opposition candidate for president. Kim Dae-jung was kidnapped because he had criticized some of Park's policies, and he was nearly killed by his abductors. Kim Dae-jung recalled the terrifying incident in 2000:

The agents took me to their boat at anchor along the seashore. They tied me up, blind[fold]ed me, and stuffed my mouth. Just when they were about to throw me overboard, Jesus Christ appeared before me with such clarity. I clung to him and begged him to save me.[23]

His wife, Lee Hee-ho, continued the story:

Suddenly [my husband] could feel even through his taped eyes a bright flash of light and a very loud noise in the sky. The kidnappers believed he was being rescued and they untied him. No one has ever been able to identify the plane which they believed to be overhead.[24]

Instead of dying by drowning, he was taken from Japan to a South Korean prison until international pressure helped reduce his sentence to house arrest. The narrow escape strengthened Kim Dae-jung's faith, which remained a central motivating force until the end of his life.

Under Park, the South Korean press and media faced severe censorship. In addition to clamping down on overt criticism of the legalized dictatorship, the known presence of a secret

23. Nobel Lecture, The Nobel Foundation, 10 December 2000.
24. *Praying for Tomorrow (Letters to My Husband in Prison)*, Lee Hee-ho, University of Southern California, 2000.

service agency running unchecked and with almost unlimited power was enough to limit freedom of speech severely.

Like Syngman Rhee before him, General Park faced a constitutional limit to the number of terms he could serve as president. And, like Rhee before him, he forced through an amendment in 1969 which allowed him to continue for a further term. He narrowly avoided defeat by Kim Dae-jung in the 1971 presidential election. Once sworn in to office, Park took steps to impose his rule permanently by declaring a state of martial law. Newspapers and broadcasters were censored and universities were closed. It was a self-coup in which he overthrew his own constitution. The National Assembly was dismissed and the constitution abolished in favour of one drawn up by Park and his inner circle.

In 1972 many of the members of the disbanded National Assembly who had been close to Kim Dae-jung were arrested. Many suffered brutal torture and some attempted suicide. Kim Dae-jung's wife, Lee Hee-ho, recalled how, "deprived of any clothing, they were mercilessly pummelled with wooden bats, deprived of sleep and had water poured into their nostrils while hanging upside-down, like so much beef hanging from hooks in the slaughter house. Listening to these stories of horror, my body shuddered with indescribable indignation and sorrow."

Many of the worst practices from the first half of the century, first perpetrated by the occupying Japanese, were now re-enacted by the South Korean regime. Lee Hee-ho described the years of house arrest, imprisonment, and persecution as "truly an Orwellian world of illegal brutality – acting as if they would never have to answer to God for their barbarity".

Like many others caught in equally cruel situations, Kim Dae-jung and Lee Hee-ho found increasing solace in their Christian faith. As Lee Hee-ho said, "In that terrible situation the only one I could turn to was the Lord… I prayed endlessly for the country and our suffering people."

Park's self-coup saw the new "Yushin" Constitution overthrow the Third Republic of South Korea and replace it with the Fourth Republic of South Korea. "Yushin" meant "rejuvenation" or "renewal" but it also hinted at "restoration", revealing that the constitution took inspiration from the imperial and industrial Meiji Restoration of Japan in the mid-1800s. Park evidently wanted to mirror the Meiji Restoration in centralizing power, modernizing the military, and bolstering the economy.

Human rights were an obstacle to be overcome in the pursuit of a greater vision for South Korea.

CHAPTER 8

Post-war South: Democracy and Recovery

As in the dark days of Japanese rule, churches welcomed pro-democracy activists, and their buildings became meeting places for the movement. The meetings were monitored by state security agents but, despite this, and showing great courage, many of those working for democracy and human rights stood up to share their stories of persecution and torture.

Christian songs, such as abolitionist James Russell Lowell's stirring 1845 hymn "Once to Every Man and Nation", became anthems for the pro-democracy movement and were sung around the country in defiance of the military government. Kim Dae-jung's wife, Lee Hee-ho, said that "whenever [Lowell's] hymn was sung by a group of people I got a great feeling of courage but also felt a mighty bond of communion. It created a great sense of joy, unity, and harmony among us."

This bold expression of political and religious freedom was bought at a heavy price. Park's government executed eight people it accused of seeking to overthrow the dictatorship, and the authorities even blocked the funeral cortège bringing the executed bodies to the church where Lee Hee-ho had gone to pray.

When the police tried to hijack the funeral car, Maryknoll priest[25] Father James Sinott lay down in front of the car with the

---

25. Maryknoll is the name shared by three Catholic mission organizations originating in the US: the Maryknoll Fathers and Brothers; the Maryknoll Sisters; and the Maryknoll Lay Missioners. Founded in 1910, Maryknoll has sent Catholic missionaries all over the world.

murdered men's widows. Lee Hee-ho recorded that the police "manhandled the priest as if he were a stray dog, kicking and beating him mercilessly".

Another Catholic priest, Moon Jung-hyon, inserted wet chewing gum into the ignition, so, after discovering that they couldn't start the engine, the police brought a crane and hoisted the funeral car off the road. They took the bodies of the executed men to a secret location, where they burned them. Lee Hee-ho said the authorities felt compelled to do this as they had learned "that Catholic Priests for Justice were going to have the bodies examined for evidence of torture".

Although Father Moon was badly injured in the stand-off and other ministers were expelled from the country, a formidable alliance of Christians had been mobilized. Seoul's Myeongdong Cathedral became a meeting place for dissidents and a regular special Mass was said for the persecuted.

In March 1976, four years after Park had disbanded the National Assembly, Lee Hee-ho encouraged the distribution of the "Declaration for Democracy and National Salvation", a courageous manifesto that pronounced a fundamental belief in democracy, demanded an end to economic subservience to Japan, and committed to national unification – "the most important task that our people will have to achieve". It asserted that democracy represented the only way to end national suffering and it proclaimed that South Korea should be "a proud and peaceful nation of justice and human rights". This was, of course, a direct threat to the authority of the Park regime.

The dictatorship responded by indicting and detaining 11 of the signatories, and seven others were indicted without detention. Kim Dae-jung was arrested yet again, along with numerous priests and ministers of many Christian denominations – the leaders of the democratic movement.

In prison, Kim Dae-jung began exchanging letters with his wife and sons. His letters have since been published and they reveal the motivations, faith, and moral courage that drove him.[26]

Lee Hee-ho wrote back, often having to hide her letters in toilet rolls to avoid confiscation. In her first letter, sent on 23 April 1977, she told him to "pass on all our difficulties to God". It was a message she would repeat again and again, also insisting that "a Christian cannot tolerate or compromise with falsehood or injustice".

In the following year, the Reverend Park Hyung-khu gave in to the regime and persuaded other indicted prisoners to sign a memorandum of penitence, admitting their treason. For Lee Hee-ho, it was like "a night of darkness; the true nadir". Her husband refused to sign the document, so communications between them became even more restricted.

The remaining years of Park's reign were characterized by an increasingly authoritarian and oppressive rule. After three years of imprisonment, in 1978, Kim Dae-jung finally returned home, though long periods of house arrest followed. He began his statement on release by offering thanks to God and insisting that "only through the restoration of democracy can we attain our national goals of freedom, justice, and national unification".

Ten months later, in October 1979, President Park was assassinated by Kim Jae-gyu, Director of Central Intelligence. Throughout his reign, Park had accumulated numerous enemies, both domestic and foreign, and he had faced assassination on a number of previous occasions. On 21 January 1968 members of Kim Il-sung's Unit 124 Special Forces Commandos had come close to assassinating Park at the Blue House. Six years later, on 15 August 1974, Park was giving a speech at the National Theatre of Korea. A Japanese-born North Korean sympathizer,

26.Kim Dae-jung, *Prison Writings*, first published 23 April 1987.

seated in the front row, drew a gun and fired on the president at close range. His first shot missed his intended target but his second shot, aimed at a bodyguard, killed Park's wife, Yuk Young-soo.

This second assassination attempt and the loss of his wife shook the soldier-president. Writing in *Time* magazine in August 1999, ex-US Ambassador to South Korea Donald Gregg reported that in November 1974 Park reflected that "had he not chosen to stand for another term in 1972, his wife might still be alive". The 1974 assassination attempt caused all diplomatic ties to be severed with Kim Il-sung's regime in North Korea.

The Yushin regime came to an end on 26 October 1979 when Park's trusted friend and KCIA director Kim Jae-gyu assassinated the president at dinner in the Blue House. Kim Jae-gyu shot Park in the chest and wounded him but, for reasons that are uncertain, he left the room and did not shoot him again for some minutes. When he returned and shot the president for a second time, the bullet entered Park's head and killed him instantly. Kim Jae-gyu's motive is still unclear. As the director of the KCIA he was well connected, powerful, and experienced in planning extremely complex missions. The disorganized assassination of President Park left many observers puzzled. Kim Jae-gyu's behaviour seemed far too careless for one so expert in planning complicated and dangerous actions.

It seems most likely that Kim Jae-gyu shot President Park partly because of repeated humiliations by Park and his chief bodyguard, Cha Ji-chul, and partly for ideological reasons. Kim Jae-gyu had clashed repeatedly with the extremist Cha over the most appropriate tactics for dealing with anti-Park sentiment in the country. Over the final years of the Park presidency, Cha had steered Park to increased levels of oppression and brutality against his own people. Though he was the head of the chief instrument of repression in South Korea, Kim Jae-gyu did not agree with the extent of the violence against civilian protesters and he took definitive action, albeit in an uncharacteristically shambolic manner. Kim Jae-gyu was later executed by hanging.

Chaos threatened South Korea in the wake of Park's death. As the serving prime minister, Choi Kyu-hah was first in line for the presidency and quickly promised genuinely democratic elections to create a new administration and a new, fairer constitution. Choi won the election in December 1979 and paved the way for the Fifth Republic of South Korea. Days later, Major-General Chun Doo-hwan staged another successful coup against Choi and took control of the government. On 17 May 1980 he declared a state of martial law and installed himself as president in the following September.

All forms of opposition were violently suppressed. The first of many came in May 1980 when Chun sent Special Forces units of the South Korean army to put down the Gwangju Democratization Movement. A massacre followed. The uprising gave Chun the excuse to implicate Kim Dae-jung, to whom the electorate in the city of Gwangju were fiercely loyal.

Kim Dae-jung was rearrested and sentenced to death for sedition and insurrection. By August he was on trial for treason, and the prosecutors, having interrogated him for 60 days, demanded the most severe sentence. In September his sons followed him to jail. Lee Hee-ho said, "My heart ached with grief. Confronted by the overwhelming reality I couldn't even cry."

Once again Kim Dae-jung stared death in the face.

At the close of his trial, Kim Dae-jung was permitted to make a statement to the court. He took his chance to call for "national reconciliation without political reprisal" and to beg the democratic activists and Park loyalists to show generosity and "co-operate for the sake of the nation".

The other defendants wept and sang the national anthem and, as they were removed from the court, they sang "We shall overcome" and chanted, "Long live Kim Dae-jung," and, "Long live our democracy." It was a brave show but had no effect on the Chun regime officials.

Confronted with her husband's imminent execution, Lee Hee-ho suffered terribly. "My hair fell out in bundles," she said later. She began writing letters to world leaders, including French President François Mitterrand, German statesman Willy Brandt and US President Ronald Reagan. She urged a nationwide campaign of prayer, which was taken up in other parts of the world and, before long, "a powerful movement was afoot to save my husband".

Every day for the first six months he was in prison, Kim Dae-jung expected death. He was saved once more from political assassination when both Pope John Paul II and the US government intervened. The Pope wrote to Chun in December 1980, urging clemency for the Catholic Kim. Negotiations by the US Reagan Administration succeeded in reducing the death sentence to a 20-year term and, by 1982, Kim Dae-jung was allowed to live in exile in America. For the time being, he was out of Korean politics.

As in Park's era, South Korea's industrial and export economy flourished under Chun's single-minded military junta. However, unlike during the previous presidency, the gap between the rich and the ordinary citizens grew. Whereas Park had succeeded in lifting entire communities out of poverty with his "New Community Movement" and numerous five-year plans, Chun inflicted a despotic rule on South Korea. Poverty increased among the rural poor and the freedoms of speech and of the press were further curtailed. Universities were closed to keep down the revolutionary-minded students.

Chun's reign came to an end in 1988 when the country erupted in protest after the Catholic Priests Association for Justice revealed that his administration had tortured a Seoul

University student to death. Chun's Democratic Justice Party set the date for democratic presidential elections and Chun stood down to make way for his chosen successor, ex-General Roh Tae-woo. The deeply unpopular Roh faced two formidable opponents in Kim Dae-jung and Kim Young-sam; luckily for him, neither of the Kims would stand aside for the other and the opposition vote was split between them. Roh became president by the narrowest of margins.

President Roh was only too aware of his tenuous grip on power. He promised and actually delivered true democratic reform and renewed efforts towards meaningful diplomacy with North Korea. Though he was later tried and duly convicted for the part he played in the Gwangju Massacre, it was Roh Tae-woo who broke the succession of military dictatorships and delivered a permanent democracy to South Korea.

In 1993 he was beaten in the ballot by the well-known anti-corruption politician Kim Young-sam. The new president threw the full weight of the law at the surviving leaders of South Korea's authoritarian regimes, jailing Chun and Roh for corruption and treason. Both men served time in jail until they were pardoned by the outgoing Kim Young-sam on the advice of President-elect Kim Dae-jung, who took office in 1998. Kim Dae-jung's intervention in the disgraced presidents' cases was all the more remarkable because of the death sentence Chun had imposed on him 20 years earlier.

The outgoing Kim Young-sam government faced grave economic problems as the Asian economic downturn plunged South Korea and its neighbours into near-bankruptcy. When Kim Dae-jung took office, the country was approaching a financial cliff edge. His reforms promoted fairness and accountability in trade and government, and he ended government cronyist subsidies to large corporations. The economy shrank by almost 6 per cent in his first year, but grew by over 10 per cent in his second, and South Korea came back from the brink of economic ruin.

Kim Dae-jung's remarkable presidency was defined in part by "the Sunshine Policy" – explored in chapter 11 – which signalled a change of direction in the South's engagement with the hostile dictatorship of North Korea. The Sunshine Policy took its name from a fable by Aesop, in which a show of strength by the proud North Wind fails to remove a traveller's heavy cloak. Only the warmth of the benevolent sun succeeds in persuading the man to take off his outer layers.

On 15 June 2000, President Kim met Chairman Kim in Pyongyang in an historic meeting.

"I went with a heavy heart not knowing what to expect," Kim Dae-jung said later that year, "but convinced that I must go for the reconciliation of my people and peace on the Korean peninsula. There was no guarantee that the summit meeting would go well. Divided for half a century after a three-year war, South and North Korea have lived in mutual distrust and enmity across the barbed-wire fence of the demilitarized zone."

When they signed the cordial North–South Joint Declaration, it seemed for a moment that the North Korean traveller was showing signs that he was about to take off his coat.

CHAPTER 9

Post-war North: *Songun, Juche,* and the Cult of Personality

By the late 1950s, Kim Il-sung was already rewriting both his own past and the history of Communism in Korea to magnify his achievements. He engaged the help of Soviet-educated Korean Hwang Jang-yop to go over his past speeches and erase any deferential reference to Stalin and Russian Communism.

The speeches were just the beginning, and a thorough rewrite of Korean history got under way. Previously mandatory books on Marx, Engels, and Lenin were banned, and the names and achievements of other prominent Korean Communists disappeared from party records. Kim Il-sung was left as the sole originator of Korean Communism and the founder of the Korean Communist Party. His war record was also transformed into a series of legendary victories over the "American imperialists", culminating in his driving them back into the south.

Even his family history was rewritten to increase his personal glory. The new account claimed it was Kim Il-sung's great-grandfather who had heroically captured the US trading ship *General Sherman* in 1866.

During the work, Hwang came across a speech Kim Il-sung had delivered to the party in December 1955 which said, "*Juche* means Chosun's revolution."[27] At the time, *Juche* was a Korean-language translation of the Stalinist concept of "the people" as a homogeneous, self-reliant unit.

---

27. Jasper Becker, *Rogue Regime: Kim Jong-il and the Looming Threat of North Korea*, OUP, 2005, p. 65.

"We decided to expand the term and add to it," Hwang Jang-yop wrote later. "We then agreed to interpret it as every [decision and policy] in the north should be decided in conformity with Chosun's reality and in the interests of the Chosun people."[28]

In practice, it was "Chosun's reality" that had to keep adjusting in line with party policy. *Juche* became the spearhead of Kim Il-sung's campaign to reject all foreign influence on North Korean society and establish a Mao-style cult of personality for himself. Therefore the new Communist history declared that "the Dear Leader", as a brilliant teenager, had invented *Juche* in the 1930s and that the policy was now hailed as a stroke of political and social genius by a jealous world.[29]

Though *Juche*'s real inventor was Hwang Jang-yop, it is believed by outside observers that Kim Il-sung and his son, Kim Jong-il, took an active role in developing and expanding it. In 1965, Kim Il-sung defined the three pillars of *Juche* as political independence, economic self-sufficiency, and self-reliance in defence. In 1982, Kim Jong-il published *On the Juche Idea*, which established him, after his father, as the highest interpreter of the policy.

Juche began as a five-year plan from 1956 to 1961 that focused on the rapid economic development of heavy industry. The goal was to rebuild quickly in the wake of the destructive Korean War and to ensure independence from foreign powers, even including the Communist allies of Russia and China.

Independence remained an elusive goal for the DPRK, and economic aid from the Soviet bloc propped up the unbalanced North Korean economy. With such a disproportionate emphasis on industry, a number of staple domestic supplies and consumer goods became scarce.

---

28. Becker, *Rogue Regime*, p. 66.
29. As I relate in chapter 13, the *Juche* philosophy – along with Pyongyang's Juche Tower, which celebrates it – is in need of urgent repair.

By the mid-1980s, North Korea was unable to feed itself. The ponderous administration and the lack of technological advancement inhibited the production of food. When the USSR failed in 1991, and the Soviet bloc dissolved thereafter, the DPRK regime lost its long-standing ally, a host of trading partners, and its primary source of economic and food aid. The Hermit Kingdom, with its isolationist policies, really was alone. The North Korean economy nosedived. The DPRK government responded by increasing the quantity of labour demanded from workers, reducing wages, and cutting food allowances under the Two Meals A Day campaign.

China stepped in to supply the shortfall left by the collapse of the Soviet Union and, by 1993, was supplying an astonishing 68 per cent of North Korea's food. When China's own grain shortages hit home, they severed the aid lifeline to the DPRK and famine ravaged North Korea. The most intense suffering came between 1994 and 1998, when an estimated 3.5 million people died. The catastrophic floods of 1995 were much to blame, washing away farms, fields, and infrastructure, as well as destroying the underground grain stores that held the country's emergency supplies. Energy production failed and water sources were contaminated.

On 8 July 1994, quite unrelated to his country's dire situation, Kim Il-sung suffered a sudden heart attack and died shortly afterwards. After the traditional Confucian period of mourning, Kim Jong-il succeeded his father as leader of North Korea.

Three years later, the architect of *Juche*, Hwang Jang-yop, walked into the South Korean Embassy in Beijing and defected. The event became an international incident, and the embassy was quickly surrounded by Chinese police. Eventually, the Chinese authorities allowed Hwang to defect to South Korea via the Philippines. On his defection, his wife committed suicide and one of his daughters died in unusual circumstances, when she fell from a lorry. Fred Kaplan, writing for American political website Slate, reported that at least two of Hwang's other children were sent to forced labour camps.[30]

Hwang died in October 2010 aged 87, and is the highest-ranking DPRK defector to date. He remained devoted to the cause of *Juche* as he understood it, and accused Kim Jong-il of building feudalism instead of socialism.

When Kim Jong-il succeeded his father, he was not the most senior member of government; others were above him. Nor was he the most senior figure in the military. The KPA was still his strongest and closest source of support and so he consolidated his own standing by increasing the power of the military. As part of his effort to become the undisputed leader of the DPRK, Kim Jong-il made an additional amendment to *Juche*: the 1996 inclusion of the policy of *Songun*.

Songun means "military first". The policy bought Kim Jong-il the loyalty of the army by elevating the KPA to the position of first priority in decision-making and application of resources. It also promoted the KPA as the perfect model for civilian society to emulate; as a forerunner of *Songun*, the 31 years of Kim Il-sung's *Juche* had prepared the North Korean people to submit to authority without question.

The *Songun* period is "officially" dated from 25 August 1960, when a young Kim Jong-il accompanied his father on a visit to the Seoul 105th Guards Armoured Division Headquarters in Pyongyang. The DPRK claims that Kim Jong-il gave "on-the-spot advice" to the tank unit, which "brought about a turning point in developing the revolutionary armed forces and accomplishing the revolutionary cause of *Juche*". The regime prioritized military might as a core part of the self-sufficiency and reliance policy of *Juche*, but the term *Songun* did not appear

30. Fred Kaplan, "The Pyongyang Candidate", www.slate.com, 30 October 2003.

in official government policy or documentation for over 30 years.

By 1998, the word was in regular use by the DPRK leadership to create and describe new party terminology, such as *Songun* politics, *Songun* leadership, and the *Songun* revolutionary feats. The practice is still ongoing. The DPRK's Korean Central News Agency (KCNA) claims that the late Kim Jong-il started "the *songun* revolutionary leadership with perfect traits and qualifications as a brilliant commander", and he "performed undying exploits... with his outstanding ideas and extraordinary leadership".

The KCNA also claims, somewhat anachronistically, that Kim Il-sung demonstrated *Songun* leadership in the "defeat" of the USA at the end of the Korean War: "The historic victory in the Fatherland Liberation War was the brilliant fruition of the immortal *Songun* idea and exploits of *Songun* leadership of President Kim Il-sung."

Juche and *Songun* continue to make headlines at the KCNA. In 2008 it reported that a seminar on the *Juche* idea was held in Ethiopia, and a film about the 75th anniversary of "the Heroic Korean People's Army" was screened in Uzbekistan. Neither event occurred. On 8 January 2009 Kenichi Ogami, the Secretary-General of the International Institute of the Juche Idea, praised the "spirit of the people of the DPRK" and stated that "world progressives are watching Korea [with] envy". The "international" institute is based entirely within the DPRK.

More recently, on 12 June 2012, the KCNA reported that the Brazilian Centre for the Study of the Juche Idea was inaugurated at São Paulo University in Brazil. It was, of course, fictitious. The imaginary chairman declared, "We will widely organize colourful events to grandly commemorate the centenary of [the] birth of President Kim Il-sung, the founder of the Juche idea and the father of socialist Korea, in close touch with regional and international Juche idea study organizations."

The DPRK and the Korean Central News Agency even claim there are groups active in the United Kingdom, including the Juche Idea Study Group in Britain, the UK Association for the Study of Songun Politics, the Society for Unity and Independence of England, and the Anglo-Peoples Korea Friendship Association. It claims there are many *Juche*-devotee diaspora groups across the world, in what the very real Peterson Institute for International Economics calls "fictionalised internationalism".

Unfortunately, not all of the DPRK's internationalism is fictional. The application of *Songun* had the very real-world result of establishing the Korean People's Army as a formidable force. Today the KPA is the fourth-largest standing army in the world, with 1.1 million soldiers in active service, supported by an additional 8.2 million reservists. This represents 38 per cent of a total population of 24.4 million people. The KPA has a policy of conscription, with a service length of between three and five years, the aim of which is to train the citizenry in combat and taking orders from the hierarchy. The soldiers have the standing order of keeping the world at bay.

The KPA forces are divided between a conventional ground force, a navy, and an air force, with additional divisions in the forms of the Strategic Rocket Forces and the North Korean Special Operation Force. The Strategic Rocket Forces division has proved especially useful to the regime in its engagement with the international community. The US Institute for Science and International Security estimates that the DPRK possesses enough materials to build up to nine nuclear warheads. Combined with the advent of the Rodong-1 ballistic missile, test-fired into the Sea of Japan in 1993 and again in 2003, the destructive capabilities of the North Korean regime were intimidating to say the least. With the 2012 launch of the Unha-3 rocket, which succeeded in putting a satellite into space, the threat of North Korea achieving an intercontinental ballistic missile became even more urgent.

When the isolationist *Juche* is combined with the might-is-right *Songun*, the result is a government determined to outgun the world. Now, following the successful test of a nuclear device on 12 February 2013 – one which the North Korean Central News Agency originally claimed was "miniaturised", implying it could be fitted to a missile – the stakes are higher than ever. Following the worldwide coverage of the event, the KCNA amended their press release to say the device was "smaller" rather than miniaturised, but the damage was already done.[31]

North Korea is the only country in the world to have withdrawn from the Treaty on the Non-Proliferation of Nuclear Weapons, which it originally signed on 12 December 1985. North Korea had made significant threats to withdraw in 1993, but changed its position before the withdrawal came into effect. After the 1993 crisis was resolved, the 1994 Agreed Framework brought North Korea back to the negotiating table in an agreement in which the US promised food and fuel aid and the construction of two thermal "light water" reactors in exchange for an end to North Korea's plutonium enrichment programme.

On 10 April 2003, the DPRK finally abandoned the treaty. A DPRK source later announced that they had withdrawn their signature because of the need to manufacture "nuclear arms for self-defence to cope with the Bush administration's ever-more undisguised policy to isolate and stifle the DPRK". On 9 October 2006 the United States Geological Survey detected a seismic event in North Korea equivalent to a 4.3 magnitude earthquake – indicating a successful nuclear test. More recently, on 12 February 2013, another powerful tremor was detected. This was followed by confirmation of another successful nuclear test by the DPRK leadership in their statement: "The test was carried out as part of practical measures of counteraction to defend the country's security and sovereignty in the face of the ferocious hostile act of

31. www.kcna.co.jp/item/2013/201302/news12/20130212-18ee.html

the US which wantonly violated the DPRK's legitimate right to launch satellite for peaceful purposes."[32]

Now North Korea's arsenal includes the full array of weapons of mass destruction: a plutonium-based nuclear weapons programme supplemented by uranium enrichment; the world's third largest chemical weapons arsenal; possible biological weapons; and a range of ballistic missiles.

This has caused a great deal of anxiety in South Korea and around the world, and – combined with the increasingly well-documented government repression of its own suffering people – the North Korean regime has been frequently labelled as an irrational actor and a loose nuclear cannon. The Six-Party Talks,[33] aimed at resolving the ongoing nuclear crisis, failed to win major behavioural changes from the Kim regime, and more recent sanctions seem to have spurred them on.

In fact, the DPRK leadership have shown themselves to be anything but irrational in their management of the six-party negotiations. Jim Picht, a journalist writing in the *Washington Times*,[34] pointed out that a truly irrational actor would not have manipulated the process with such breathtaking success as the DPRK has done.

The upper echelon of the North Korean regime has benefited enormously from the repeated cycle of provocation, sanctions, isolation, and renegotiation. The DPRK's presence at the renewed talks has always been bought at a heavy price in dollars and supplies, which go directly to the Kim family and their circle of supporters.

Kim Jong-un's ascension to party leadership on 28 December 2011 appeared to bring some positive signs. In February

32. www.kcna.co.jp/item/2013/201302/news12/20130212-18ee.html
33. Involving North Korea, China, South Korea, Russia, Japan, and America.
34. "The rational madness of North Korea", *Washington Times*, 27 November 2010.

2012 North Korea announced it would suspend nuclear tests and allow inspectors from the International Atomic Energy Agency (IAEA) to monitor uranium enrichment activities. This concession was, of course, bought with further pledges of food aid, but following the nuclear test of 12 February 2013, it is now sadly clear that this was just another well-managed cycle of talks and payments.

Kim Jong-un has begun to make his mark on the twin policies of *Juche* and *Songun*, having already fused them into the joint doctrine of "Kimilsungism-Kimjongilism", which, predictably, the KCNA reports is now being studied by enthusiastic scholars and statesmen across the world. The KCNA published an article on its website dating the formation of Kimilsungism-Kimjongilism by "dear respected" Kim Jong-un as 6 April 2012.

The typically revisionist article noted that "the Korean people have long called the revolutionary ideas of the President [Kim Il-sung] and Kim Jong-il as Kimilsungism-Kimjongilism and recognized it as the guiding idea [of the nation]". The KCNA has also made frequent references to the twin policies under the singular title of "the great guiding idea". The two policies have become one and the DPRK's rewriting of history continues.

CHAPTER 10

The Gulags of North Korea

Confronted by the degradations and humiliations experienced by Kim Dae-jung and South Korea's democracy activists, I am always struck by the dignity with which they responded. They refused to let their spirits be crushed and never lost hope. I am also struck by how rapidly things changed and dictatorship gave way to a vibrant, open democracy, creating one of the finest nations in the world. Kim Dae-jung, who was instrumental in this transformation, was able to forgive his torturers and knew that cycles of revenge, where an eye is claimed for an eye, merely leave everyone blind. It is worth reflecting on this when thinking about the past and present suffering in the North and how things might be one day.

Learning to forgive does not, however, mean learning to forget.

Since the establishment of the 1948 Universal Declaration of Human Rights, the history of the intervening 60 years has illustrated both the possibilities and the limitations of making progress on human rights questions. In places such as Rwanda, South Sudan, Darfur, the Congo, and Somalia, the international community dismally failed to prevent genocide and crimes against humanity. But there has been significant progress in other areas – ranging from the use of torture, slavery, trafficking, and the treatment of minorities and refugees to women's rights and children's rights. The fall of the Berlin Wall, the Velvet Revolution of 1989, the ending of apartheid, and the democratization of the Philippines and South Korea during the same decade all serve to demonstrate how human rights concerns can powerfully shape the politics of entire regions.

North Korea is a signatory to four international human rights treaties: the International Covenant on Civil and Political Rights, the International Covenant on Economic, Social, and Cultural Rights, the Convention on the Rights of the Child, and the Convention on the Elimination of All Forms of Discrimination against Women. Constantly asking North Korea how it honours its treaty obligations would be a good start to raising the subject but its treatment of civilians in its prison camps should always be the top priority.

In 2012 I was privileged to spend time with Mr Kim Sang-hun and Dr Yoon Yeo-sang and staff working at the Database Centre for North Korean Human Rights (NKDB). They have made it their mission to ensure that, whatever happens in the future, the world will never forget the stories of those who have endured so much suffering in the prison camps of the North.

NKDB was established in 2003 to push human rights concerns up the international agenda and to seek restitution for human rights violations in the past. Everyone who escapes from the North is carefully and systematically interviewed and their stories recorded in great detail. I spent time with some of those engaged in this painstaking but crucial work. By collecting data, analysing human rights incidents, assisting victims, recording case notes, dealing with post-traumatic stress disorder, and publishing empirical and evidence based reports, NKDB has used internationally accepted and standardized methods.

In 2007 they created the North Korean Human Rights Archives and in 2012 they published a white paper based on the histories contained in 42,408 cases. This comprises 35,778 accounts based on personal experience or as eyewitnesses and 6,630 from second-hand or other sources. The personal profiles of 23,437 people are now held in the archive – and these include the testimonies of more than 20,000 victims (who now reside in South Korea), the admissions of 864 perpetrators, and the narratives of 2,111 witnesses. During my visit I met a recent defector who had himself been involved in committing crimes against civilians held in prison camps.

In meeting victims I have been particularly moved by the dignity, integrity, and bearing of those who have endured and lived to tell their tales of the horrors of North Korea. On a number of occasions, and again in 2012, I have met Shin Dong-hyok, whose harrowing story is told by Blaine Harden in *Escape from Camp 14* – extracts of which were broadcast by BBC Radio Four – and it would be impossible not to be deeply affected by both his story and his demeanour. Despite everything that has been done to him and his family, he still loves his country and wants the best for North Korea and its people.

Twenty-six-year-old Shin spent the first 23 years of his life in North Korea's Political Prison Camp 14, where he was born. Camp 14 is one of five sprawling prison camps in the mountains of North Korea, about 90 kilometres north of Pyongyang. No one born in Camp 14 or any other political prison camp within the "absolute control zone" had ever before escaped from North Korea. These are places where the hard labour, the malnutrition, and freezing conditions – minus 20 degrees Celsius in winter – will kill you long before you could ever get in front of the firing squad.

According to Shin, men and women perceived by the authorities to be good workers are arbitrarily selected by prison guards and permitted – or rather forced – to get married, with a view to producing children who will become model workers. Children born in the prison camp are treated as prisoners from birth. Shin was one such child.

Shin told my parliamentary committee that he was forced to work from the age of 10 or 11 and, as a child, he had witnessed unthinkable horrors, including fellow child prisoners being beaten to death. He told me that children and parents were required to watch and report on one another and Shin was interrogated in an underground torture chamber after some of his family members tried to escape from the camp. Following this failed escape attempt, he was forced, on 6 April 1996, to watch as his mother and brother were publicly executed – a common practice in the camps.

The brutality did not stop there: guards bound the hands and feet of the 13-year-old Shin and roasted him over a fire. The burns still scar his back just as the memories have indelibly scarred his mind, and he remains haunted by the double life he was forced to lead and the lies he had to tell to survive.

"Afterwards, my father and I could not mingle with other prisoners and we had to work even harder than the rest," he said.

On another occasion, Shin was assigned to work in a garment factory. Severe hard labour is a common feature of North Korea's prison camps. He accidentally dropped a sewing machine, and as a punishment the prison guards chopped off his middle finger.

Shin recalled how, when he was a child in the prison school, his teacher informed the children that they were animals whose parents should have been killed. The teacher told them that, by contrast, he was a human with every kind of right and privilege, but that they should be grateful to be alive.

Shin also recalled seeing a seven-year-old girl in his class being severely beaten because she was discovered to have picked up a few grains of wheat on the way to school. The beating continued for two hours and her classmates had to carry her home. She died the next day.

It was then that Shin encountered an inmate who had *not* spent his entire life inside Camp 14. He had seen the outside, having lived in China for a time before he fell foul of the regime on his return to North Korea. "During the time I spent with him, I learned so much about the outside world," Shin said. Then came a remarkable revelation: "I realized that this life in the camp was not the ordinary life."

In 2005, having been tortured, mistreated, and discriminated against as the son and brother of declared traitors – and suffering from constant hunger – Shin and his newly acquired friend tried to escape.

His compatriot died on the barbed wire – not realizing that it carried a strong electric current – but Shin escaped, though he was badly burned, by literally climbing over the dead body of his friend, which made his escape possible. Shin's escape was an overwhelming blend of agony and ecstasy. He recalls:

> *[I felt something] stabbing the sole of my foot when I passed through the wire. I almost fainted but, by instinct, I pushed myself forward through the fence. I looked around to find the barbed wire behind me but [my friend] was motionless, hanging over the wire fence! At that desperate moment I could afford little thought of my poor friend and I was just overwhelmed by joy. The feeling of ecstasy to be out of the camp was beyond description.*

Shin described to us first seeing the country of North Korea outside the prison camps and said that, by comparison with the prison camp, it looked like paradise. Ironically, the North Korean regime tell their population that their country *is* a paradise compared with the rest of the world.

But Shin's escape from the camp did not mean he was out of danger:

> *I had run down the mountain quite a way when I felt something wet on my legs. I was in fact bleeding from the*

wound inflicted by the barbed wire. I had no time to stop but
sometime later found a locked house in the mountains. I broke
into the house and found some food that I ate, then I left with
a small supply of rice I found in the house.

For 25 days he then travelled in secret towards the Yalu River and the border with China. Once there, he bribed the guards, using the money he had obtained from selling the rice, and escaped over the border. He travelled to Shanghai and found a way over the wall of the South Korean Consulate to claim asylum. After six months within the consular compound, he was allowed to travel to Seoul. Shin was left with deep scars, both physical and emotional.

When I met him in Seoul in 2012 he was undertaking a punishing schedule, speaking at endless meetings and ensuring that good comes out of his traumatic experiences. Shin accompanied me when I visited the Kim Dae-jung Memorial Library. He had never been there before and told me that having seen pictures of Kim Dae-jung meeting North Korean leaders he had regarded him as a collaborator but, having seen the prison clothes and letters of Korea's greatest statesman, he would regard him differently in future.

This was also a salutary reminder of how the motives of bridge-builders can easily be misinterpreted.

Shin was joined at our parliamentary hearing by Ahn Myeong-cheol, aged 37, who worked as a guard at four political prison camps – and also within the absolute control zone – between 1987 and 1994.

Ahn described how his father killed himself when he realized that he had been heard criticizing the regime. His father's death was not enough to satisfy the authorities: Ahn's mother and brothers were sent to prison camps in retaliation for the criticism. Ahn was "re-educated" and became a prison guard in the camps.

He described in vivid and harrowing detail how he'd witnessed guard dogs, imported from Russia, tear three children to pieces and how the camp warden had congratulated the guard who'd trained the dogs. He said that even when prisoners die "they are punished" because their corpses are simply left to disintegrate and rot away on the open ground.

After he escaped in 1994, Ahn published *They Are Crying for Help* and, in the Moses Room of the House of Lords, where we sat under the great paintings of Moses receiving the Ten Commandments and a painting of the Judgment of Daniel, Ahn repeated his plea to the international community not to look away from the human rights violations and crimes against humanity experienced by the North Korean people.

One day a "Daniel come to Judgment" will need all the wisdom ascribed to Daniel – and perhaps to Solomon, too – in knowing how to deal with the legacy of the violent crimes of the past. Perhaps some lessons might be learned from the 1995 Truth and Reconciliation Commission in South Africa, which was created to pursue restorative justice after the abolition of apartheid. Victims who had suffered gross violations of their human rights had their testimonies recorded and some were invited to give public statements. Perpetrators were able to avoid criminal and civil prosecution, and given an amnesty, if they provided testimonies and admissions.

A similar clean-slate process was established in Rwanda. Their "Gacaca" process and courts, which I have seen first-hand, were designed to promote post-genocidal healing and to allow the country somehow to emerge from the slaughter of up to a million Tutsi people. It has not been without its problems or critics, and Korea will have to develop its own way of dealing with the past. It will need to handle the reality of the traumatized lives of men such as Lee Young-kuk. Speaking at Westminster this defector and former prison inmate pleaded that the international community end its indifference. Lee Young-kuk had once served as part of the presidential bodyguard.

He graphically described the degrading situation in prison:

From the very first day, the guards with their rifles beat me. I was trampled on mercilessly until my legs became swollen, my eardrums were shattered, and my teeth were all broken. They wouldn't allow us to sleep from 4 a.m. till 10 p.m. and once while I was sleeping they poured water over my head. Since the conditions within the prison were poor, my head became frostbitten from the bitter cold.

As I was trying to recuperate from the previous mistreatment, they ordered me to stick out my shackled feet through a hole on my cell door, and then tortured them in almost every possible way. Not a single day passed without receiving some form of torture and agonizing experience.

Sobering accounts abound.

Lee Sung-ae told parliamentarians about how, when she was jailed, all her fingernails were pulled out, all her lower teeth were destroyed, and prison guards poured water, mixed with chillies, up her nose.

Jung Guang-il described how he was subjected to "pigeon torture": hands cuffed and tied behind his back in an excruciating position, he said he felt as though his bones were breaking through his chest. All his teeth were broken during the beatings and his weight fell from 75 to 38 kilograms.

Jeong-ai Shin was held in North Korea's Camp 15. Conditions were so perilous that 1 in 10 of the 200 inmates was dead within the year. She described a regime consisting of hard labour, starvation, and infectious diseases. She finally escaped and by a circuitous route made it to South Korea.

Kim Hye-sook was first jailed when she was just 13 because her grandfather had gone to South Korea. She spent 28 years in the prison camp; even as a child, she was forced to work in coal mines and witness public executions. Like so many, Kim Hye-sook was not incarcerated because of any crime that she had committed – it was simply guilt by association, becoming a victim of North Korea's systematic punishment of family members for up to three generations if a relative is said to have committed a "crime".

In 2011 she gave her evidence to my committee. An artist, Kim Hye-sook spoke of her incarceration in Yodok Prison Camp, where she was taken aged 18. She showed a series of her own paintings depicting the suffering she witnessed and experienced first-hand. Kim Hye-sook used the pictures to explain to the group what a normal working day in Camp 18 was like, from the manual labour undertaken by prisoners and the scarcity of food provisions to the regular public executions and even cannibalism. She wept as she spoke about the death of her son in the camp.

Listening to her evidence, Rajiv Narayan of Amnesty International told me that Kim Hye-sook's story was one of great rarity as so few dissidents escape from Camp 18. He explained that Amnesty's research shows around 50,000 people are imprisoned there but the increase in agricultural production for the camp suggests the number of prisoners might be rising. Gravely, Mr Narayan added that Amnesty International estimates that two in every five prisoners die in the camp.[35]

At the same meeting we heard from Mr Kim Joo-il. He explained that he was a political dissident who fled North Korea to settle in Britain after being forced to serve 11 years in the North Korean military before his escape in 2005. In thanking

35. Mr Narayan also screened a DVD of a film entitled *Hell Holes: North Korea's Secret Prison Camps*, which can be viewed on YouTube.

the British people for the hospitality that he and other North Koreans had experienced, he spoke of malnutrition in the camps and the tendency of the DPRK to lavish gifts on their most loyal supporters. He then showed a video of North Korean women to illustrate the level of hysteria, the use of propaganda, and indoctrination.

A third witness, Mr Ha Tae-hyung, spoke about his experiences with Open Radio for North Korea[36] and emphasized the need to provide more information about the situation in the DPRK. Explaining that communications within the DPRK were extremely restricted, he said that ownership of a mobile phone from a banned network could lead to public execution. He speculated that human rights abuses would intensify if the regime felt its power diminishing.

These accounts have come from survivors but many will never be able to tell their stories. In addition to those who have died of hunger and exhaustion in the camps, capital punishment has been used routinely. And the situation has not been getting better: 52 executions took place in one recent year following the failed currency reforms of December 2009, including that of the Minister of Railways, Kim Yong-sam, and Vice-Minister So Nam-sin.

On 27 September 2010 an editorial in *The Times* entitled "Slave State" powerfully summed up the situation: "The condition of the people of North Korea ranks among the great tragedies of the past century. The despotism that consigns them to that state is one of its greatest crimes."

One of the most upsetting accounts I have heard in regard to the DPRK camps is the story of Lee Keumsoon, a young woman who was deported back to North Korea from China in 2004. She was arrested and "repatriated" after crossing the

36. A South Korea-based NGO broadcasting over North Korea english.nkradio.org

border illegally. Her tragic story adds yet another dimension of horror to the DPRK's record on human rights and emphasizes why human rights must become a central question in our dealings with the North Korean regime.

Lee Keumsoon was a young woman whose precise age remains unknown. She originated from Hamgyeongbuk-do Undok in the far north-east of North Korea and crossed the border, hoping to earn some money to improve her life back home. While she was in China she became pregnant.

A central tenet of North Korean ideology is belief in the purity of its blood line – a racial ideology which it holds in common with the blood-based nationalism of the Japanese colonial period. Becoming pregnant by a Chinese man (or any foreigner) is seen as a contamination of the blood line. Women who are pregnant when they are returned to North Korea know that they face forced abortion.

Lee Keumsoon attempted to hide her pregnancy while serving her prison sentence at the DPRK's Cheongjin-si Province police holding camp in North Hamgyong Province. In August 2004, after working long hours of forced labour on the construction of the Seongmak power station, and subsisting on paltry rations, she experienced a significant deterioration in her health. When the work party's supervisor sent Lee to carry stones from the river bed, she drowned in the river's strong current, swollen as it was by the summer monsoon.

Witnesses, one of whom later fled to South Korea, made a statement about these events in 2011 and said that when fellow inmates recovered Lee's corpse from the river and stripped the body, they discovered that she was wearing several layers of clothing and had a kudzu rope wound tightly around her stomach to hide her growing pregnancy. The witness said, "She didn't even tell her fellow prisoners… because they are, without exception, aborted if they don't hide it."

Following Lee's death, the camp guards forced all the female prisoners to strip off their clothes to establish whether or not they were also pregnant. The witness confirmed these measures were taken to discover pregnant women and force abortion on them.

Throughout the hearings I have chaired I have been struck by the consistent picture that has emerged of appalling violence against women in detention facilities and the chilling accounts of life in prisons and labour camps. The individual stories bring home the enormity of the suffering that lies behind individual statistics. The crucial work of the NKDB will act as a rebuke to anyone who, in the future, tries to minimize the suffering experienced by those held in the gulags, or who offers a revisionist view of these events. Good stewardship of the history of North Korea's suffering population is vital to protecting the future and healing the past.

The international community, which for so long has appeared indifferent to the fate of women like Lee Keumsoon, should remind itself of Dietrich Bonhoeffer's warning that "silence in the face of evil is itself evil" and his remark that "we have been the silent witnesses to evil deeds".

The horrific reality faced by ordinary North Koreans is now too well-documented for the world to look away and keep silent. An estimated 200,000 people are trapped in a network of gulags and camps. The testimonies of survivors leave the world with no opportunity to assert plaintively that it did not know. But first-hand witness accounts such as those of Shin Dong-hyok are a clue to the mass of evidence pointing to serial crimes against humanity, and now voices other than those of exiled North Koreans are calling for action.

The journalist Sue Lloyd-Roberts showed her brilliant BBC documentary *On the Border* to the North Korea Parliamentary Group. It is a harrowing account of those who try to leave. Mike

Kim also documents many remarkable stories in his book *Escaping North Korea*. David Hawk's *The Hidden Gulag*, Christian Solidarity Worldwide's *North Korea: A Case to Answer, A Call to Act*, and two reports by the international law firm DLA Piper commissioned by former Czech president Vaclav Havel, former Norwegian prime minister Kjell Magne Bondevik, and Holocaust survivor and Nobel Laureate Elie Wiesel, have all been pushing human rights in North Korea higher up the agenda.

Professor Vitit Muntarbhorn, the UN's Special Rapporteur on North Korea from 2004 to 2010, estimates that 400,000 people have died in North Korea's prison camps in the last 30 years. He also believes that some 300,000 people have fled the country, many of whom have died in the attempt as they make the perilous journey into China across the Tumen River.

Professor Muntarbhorn described to my parliamentary hearing how North Korea's human rights record was "abysmal" owing to "the repressive nature of the power base: at once cloistered, controlled and callous". "The exploitation of ordinary people", he said, "has become the pernicious prerogative of the ruling elite."

All eight of Muntarbhorn's reports to the UN detailed an extraordinarily grave situation. He has repeatedly said that the abuses in DPRK camps are "both systematic and pervasive" and "egregious and endemic", and he has called on the international community to "mobilize the totality of the United Nations to promote and protect human rights in the country, and accountability for human rights violations, and end impunity". In his final report, the outgoing Special Rapporteur concluded:

> *The human rights situation in this country can be described as* sui generis *– "in a category of its own"… Simply put, there are many instances of human rights violations which are both harrowing and horrific… It is thus essential to*

mobilize the United Nations and all its affiliates to act in a
more concerted manner.

At the very minimum, parliamentarians from the free parliaments of the world should form committees like Westminster's and give platforms to hear directly from those who have suffered. Such a move would end the "quietism" that has characterized international engagement with North Korea on the critical subject of human rights violations.

The atrocities can no longer be ignored if the world is talking about them.

CHAPTER 11

The Sunshine Policy

As we have seen, during his presidency of the Republic of Korea (1998–2003) Kim Dae-jung initiated the Sunshine Policy, aimed at warming the frosty relationship between North and South Korea. He believed the policy might, through a gradual process of reconciliation, lead to the reunification of the war-torn Korean peninsula.

Kim Dae-jung was immediately attacked by the Bush Administration in America and by opponents in South Korea for even trying to engage with the North. He responded by pointing out that President Nixon had embarked on diplomacy with China when that country was designated a war criminal. He reminded them that Ronald Reagan had opened a dialogue with the Soviet Union even though he had described it as "the Evil Empire". He pointed out that dialogue ultimately succeeded in restoring US–Vietnamese relations where napalm had failed.

"The United States objects to talking directly to North Korea – I cannot agree," he insisted, adding that "the only way to resolve these conflicts is through dialogue".

He pledged that the South would not seek to annex or invade the North, and that he would work to soften North Korean attitudes via economic engagement and commerce. Peaceful co-existence was Kim Dae-jung's mantra and he rejected the alternative policy of aggressive regime change. This policy did not imply weakness or appeasement, because Kim Dae-jung made it perfectly clear that armed provocation would lead to retaliation.

The two states had been at loggerheads since 1953 and Kim Dae-jung knew the stalemate would have to end, for better or worse. All that the stand-off had achieved was to push North Korea into maintaining a vast arsenal of military hardware and a huge standing army and, given its failing system of food production, the health and well-being of ordinary people had been sacrificed as a result. Decades of stalemate had brought isolation, hunger, and economic collapse to Kim Dae-jung's northern countrymen, to say nothing of the oppressive state structures controlling every part of their lives.

Against this background, Kim Dae-jung and Kim Jong-il met in Pyongyang in 2000 – the first summit since the peninsula had been finally divided at the 38th Parallel almost 50 years earlier. In October 2000, following the summit, it was said that British Prime Minister Tony Blair overruled his Foreign Secretary, Robin Cook, by announcing that Britain was normalizing relations with North Korea because, for Britain, the war was over. Addressing South Korean businessmen, Tony Blair paid tribute to Kim Dae-jung, welcoming progress towards peace on the Korean peninsula:

> *I have no doubt that we have witnessed an historic breakthrough over the last months, one that will improve the lives of all the people of the Korean peninsula, that will make Korea a stronger country and the world a safer place. I support fully President Kim's commitment to reconciliation with North Korea. That task of reconciliation in Korea is immense. Just the absence of conflict is not enough. We have to go further – spreading prosperity, building confidence, bringing people and families together, banishing the prospect of war for ever.*

Announcing the opening of an embassy in London and the restoration of diplomatic relations, Robin Cook said, "We believe that dialogue and negotiations are the best ways of securing peace and stability on the Korean peninsula."

Sunshine had only just begun and – apparently keen to prove that the ice had not melted – a North Korean source commented, "At last the imperialist hyenas whom Cook represents have been forced by the steadfastness of the DPRK and its refusal to succumb to imperialist bullying and threats to come round to the position that the DPRK has been advocating since its very inception. Better late than never!"

It was, in its way, an acknowledgment that Britain's state of war had formally ended and a new phase of engagement had begun. Despite the knee-jerk rebuttal from the North, in the eight years following the North–South summit many significant attempts at economic co-operation, tourism, and the reunion of families divided since the war were made.

There were other innovations, notably Kaesŏng Industrial Park. A collaborative economic development between North and South, it was located 10 kilometres north of the DMZ. It was initiated in 2003 and has direct rail and road access to the South. Four tax and accountancy agreements were ratified during the same year and the industrial park opened in 2004.

Chung Ju-yung, the founder of Hyundai, also constructed a resort at Mount Kumgang on North Korea's east coast and there were some significant political developments accompanying this.

The Sunshine Policy led directly to international re-engagement with North Korea and allowed a DPRK diplomatic presence in the major cities of the hated "imperialist" Western powers. This enabled previously blinkered North Korean officials to see the benefits of democracy, social freedom, and functioning market economies for themselves. A reciprocal diplomatic presence in Pyongyang also enabled useful dialogue and on-the-ground assessment of the prevailing political culture.[37]

In addition to government activity, the Sunshine Policy enabled greater travel opportunities for students, allowing for discourse, the dissemination of ideas, and a broadening of perspectives. In the dark days of the Japanese occupation and, later, the Park and Chun dictatorships, it had been students who held the oppressive authorities' feet to the fire and fought so courageously for greater political freedom. With an increased number of North Korean students learning English and experiencing the world outside the DPRK, perhaps they may return home to work for change again.

In September 2003, during my first visit to North Korea, Baroness Cox and I met South Korean pastors who were then visiting Pyongyang. We saw evidence of long-term development projects which were increasing crop yields and feeding the populace. We were able to raise human rights, security, and humanitarian issues – and explain why we believed these were pressing concerns that North Korea needed to address.

Regrettably, the Sunshine Policy did not last. Although Kim Dae-jung's successor, Roh Moo-hyun, sustained the policy with some success in commercial and joint industrial projects, the undeniable reality of DPRK nuclear tests, missile launches, military skirmishes, and President Bush's denunciation of the North as part of an "axis of evil" meant that by 2008 the Sunshine Policy was being sorely tested. By 2009 the sun had set and a new chill engulfed the peninsula; the year-old South Korean government under Lee Myung-bak pronounced the policy a failure. Kim Dae-jung died in the August of that year.

---

37. This interaction led to a meeting with the DPRK's first ambassador, Ri Yong-ho, who had complained about comments I had made in Parliament about North Korea. This resulted in Baroness Caroline Cox and myself visiting North Korea, publishing reports, and forming a parliamentary group.

The Sunshine Policy was not without its weaknesses, and President Lee argued that the government's approach had exacerbated them. He argued that it had not helped oppressed North Koreans but instead had bolstered the regime. In place of sunshine, Lee preferred the bitter winds, the posturing, and the rhetoric of the Cold War. His antipathy to the reunification agenda and lack of interest in North–South dialogue was made clear by his announcement that the Unification Ministry would close. Though he used the DPRK's human rights record as a reason for disengagement, Lee's change of policy meant the people of North Korea really were left friendless and unprotected under a hostile home government.

It can be reasonably argued that the Sunshine Policy did succeed in melting some of the surface frost, but the criticisms regarding human rights are, unfortunately, compelling. Regrettably, Kim Dae-jung's "slow but steady" agenda had little impact on human rights and faltered on security issues. Sadly, without taking the policy further, we will never know whether the initial hopes for a political "climate change" in the North were legitimate or unrealistic.

The policy also became mired in accusations of paying tribute money to appease an aggressive neighbour – and it was said that payments of several hundred million dollars were involved. Some critics branded payments for co-operation as naïve; others said it rewarded aggression. Some suggested that the North Koreans had become accomplished at selling the same horse twice and even three times over – and still not settling the account.

Following Tony Blair's decision to create diplomatic relations, James E. Hoare was appointed British Chargé d'affaires in Pyongyang. By April 2010, he was scathing in his response to Lee's criticisms of the Sunshine Policy:

Neither Kim nor Roh were starry-eyed and neither expected that the North would be changed overnight. Both responded to Pyongyang's bad behaviour with firmness. But they realized that circumstances had changed with the famine and other problems that hit North Korea in the 1990s... Perhaps some of the assistance provided was diverted away from its original purpose, but enough rice and fertilizer bags reached areas far away from Pyongyang [and the] ruling elite. Slowly, the policy was creating a group of people who could see benefits in remaining on good terms with South Korea and who had wider links with the outside world.[38]

Hoare's final assessment of discontinuing the Sunshine Policy was unequivocal: "There was never going to be a speedy change in attitudes built up over 60 years, but stopping the process after ten was not a wise decision."

My own criticism of the Sunshine Policy is that it laid insufficient emphasis on opening up the debate about what it means to be human, and the duties that every state has to uphold the human dignity and freedom of each of its citizens. The Sunshine Policy was not nearly robust enough in this area – but it was a start in the vital effort to break down the walls dividing the people of the Korean peninsula, and for that it must be recognized as a remarkable achievement.

Though this first attempt at engagement was not successful, the answer to finding a way towards a safer, productive, and more humane North Korea does not lie in a return to frosty disengagement. Turning our backs on the needs of the North Korean people is to confuse people with ideology and human needs with systems.

---

38. James E. Hoare, "Why the Sunshine Policy Made Sense", 38 North, Washington, D.C.: U.S. –Korea Institute at SAIS, Johns Hopkins University, 1 April 2010. Online at: www.38north.org/?p=188

As Aidan Foster-Carter, Honorary Senior Research Fellow in Sociology and Modern Korea at Leeds University, said in the wake of President Lee's abandonment of the policy, "Sunshine, however flawed, prised the Northern door a little ajar. Its asymmetries are easy to criticize. But does Lee Myung-bak have a better plan?"

Since the Sunshine Policy, there have been tantalizing moments during which the North and the South have encountered one another and have seen each other, and the possibilities, in a new light. In 2012 I hosted the visit to London of a South Korean doctor who runs his medical practice in the Kaesŏng joint industrial zone. He has treated over 40,000 North Korean patients. I have met an American Maryknoll priest, Father Gerry Hammond, who has made over 40 visits to North Korea on behalf of the Eugene Bell Foundation, taking in drugs and equipment to combat tuberculosis, and I have hosted two visits to the UK by the North Korean Speaker, Choe Tae-bok, and members of the North Korean Assembly, whose itinerary included open meetings with British parliamentarians and meetings with non-governmental organizations such as the Centre for Opposition Studies. None of this would have been possible without Sunshine.

As Britain and the US have learned in Iraq and Afghanistan, fragile and failing states cannot be turned around rapidly. It takes patience and perseverance: the "long haul". North Korea falls into a category all of its own and is in desperate need of a firm strategy of engagement.

Comparisons are often made with another Cold War division – East and West Germany – but they do not hold up; there is no direct parallel. Unlike North and South Korea, East and West Germany did not fight a war against one another with a colossal loss of life, and neither East nor West Germany was in a state of economic free fall or dealing with mass starvation.

The contemporary comparison of North and South Sudan is no more useful. In the case of Northern Sudan, where the country's leaders have been indicted by the International Criminal Court and are murdering their own people in a campaign of aerial bombardment, the argument for downgrading diplomatic relations and curtailing business contact with Sudan is overwhelming. This simply hasn't worked with North Korea.

The best international comparison of regime reform must surely be with Burma, a country emerging from decades of totalitarian rule through an incremental approach of diplomacy, democracy, and peace-building. And, as with that country, the process must recognize and be duly critical of the humanitarian outrages past and present.

It is intriguing to conjecture what might have happened had Kim Dae-jung's strategy been continued and the many projects that Presidents Roh Moo-hyun and Kim Jong-il agreed in 2007 been honoured. Although Kim Dae-jung's policy had its inevitable flaws – and needed greater transparency and definition – the stop–start approach which later emerged has merely left North Korea in a state of suspended animation and the peninsula as dangerous and divided a place as ever.

Internationally, political will has faltered too. In March 2009, two American journalists were arrested in North Korea. In the following November, the Korean–American Christian humanitarian Robert Park was jailed for illegal entry into the country. While these US citizens remained in captivity, it was impossible for a new diplomatic campaign to be launched by America.

The sinking of the South Korean corvette *Cheonan* in March 2010 and the shelling of Yeonpyeong Island in November 2010 by the DPRK meant no American administration – Republican or Democrat – was ever going to be able to pursue a more conciliatory policy.

After the 2012 US elections, I met in London with Ambassador Clifford A. Hart Jr, the President's Special Envoy for the Six-Party Talks, and Glyn T. Davies, the President's Special Representative for North Korea Policy. They emphasized the US Administration's desire to find ways forward but admitted to feeling deeply frustrated by what they see as North Korea's "stop–start" attempts to manipulate them. They felt equally frustrated that the Leap Day Deal of 29 February 2012 (which attempted to reopen the flow of food to North Korea) had been blown sky high by the launch of a North Korean missile. They felt it had become impossible to make any political headway in such an atmosphere.

Then, on 12 December 2012, North Korea successfully launched an Unha-3 rocket capable of putting a satellite into orbit. The US-based human rights organization LiNK[39] reported that at 00.49 a.m. (GMT) the long-range rocket "passed the island of Okinawa and debris fell into the water 300 km off the Philippines" a short time later. In response, LiNK said, South Korean President Lee Myung-bak "convened an emergency meeting with the National Security Council" while initial reports from NORAD[40] "suggested the launch may have been successful in putting a satellite in orbit".

At 3.38 p.m. GMT, I stood in the House of Lords and asked Her Majesty's Government what their assessment was of the impact on regional and world security of North Korea's recent missile launch. Baroness Warsi, the Senior Minister of State, responded by saying:

> *We condemn North Korea's satellite launch. This test of its ballistic missile technology is in clear violation of UN Security Council Resolutions 1718 and 1874. This provocative act will only serve to increase regional tensions and undermine*

---

39. Liberty in North Korea, libertyinnorthkorea.org
40. North American Aerospace Defense Command.

prospects for peace in the peninsula. The UK is urgently consulting with the UN Security Council and we have urged North Korea to return to constructive international negotiations.

Just one week before the elections in South Korea, the DPRK's timing of their launch was highly suggestive of an attempt to undermine any peaceful moves towards reconciliation and progress. I raised this point in the House and Baroness Warsi agreed: "The timing of this testing is indeed important and relevant, so soon after the US elections and the transfer of power in China and just before the elections in Japan and South Korea."

The successful launch will be viewed by the DPRK leadership as further proof of their nation's greatness, but it must be remembered that the cost of the exercise is estimated at some $800 million – a shocking waste of resources in a country where malnutrition and starvation are commonplace. A better achievement for the nation would have been to divert the funds towards feeding its people, because $800 million is enough to feed the entire population of North Korea for a year.

Encouragingly, it was not just left to Great Britain, South Korea, Japan, and the US to condemn the launch. China showed its displeasure by urging "Pyongyang [to] abide by relevant UN Security Council resolutions... which demand the DPRK not to conduct 'any launch using ballistic missile technology' and to 'suspend all activities related to its ballistic missile programme'".

Trust has been in very short supply, as those in dialogue with North Korea complain that they have heard the same promises and pledges without result. A key question remains: how do you get out of the cycle of extortion? One thing is for certain: without engagement you never will.

With new leadership in the region and the world, perhaps there might yet be another opportunity for the sun to shine on North Korea.

CHAPTER 12

Why Food Should Never Be Used as a Weapon of War

For the ordinary people of North Korea, the number-one priority is not ending the war, gaining political emancipation, or enjoying religious freedom – it is finding enough food to survive.

Since the death of Kim Jong-il in December 2011, the *Chosun Ilbo* has reported that around 20,000 people have starved to death in South Hwanghae Province alone. Tragically, this is only a small portion of the misery experienced by the North Korean people in relation to food. As many as 3.5 million people are estimated to have died during the 1990s famine (known as the Arduous March).

Despite denials from the DPRK government, the flawed policy of *Juche* is now utterly bankrupt. For decades they have failed the greatest test of self-reliance – feeding their own people. No one understands this better than Hazel Smith, Professor of Security and Resilience at Cranfield University, an expert on the dangers of famine and malnutrition[41] and North Korea.

Speaking at a meeting that I convened at Westminster, Professor Smith spelled out the chronic failure of the North Korean system. She said:

---

41. Hazel Smith is the UK's leading expert on food and agriculture in the DPRK. Between 1998 and 2002 she worked for the World Food Programme, UNDP, and UNICEF, spending around two years in North Korea, and is author of *Hungry for Peace: International Security, Humanitarian Assistance and Social Change in North Korea* (2005) and *Reconstituting Korean Security: A Policy Primer* (2007).

The [DPRK] state only provides food for key workers like miners and the military – and very occasionally welfare food to vulnerable groups like the elderly and children. As a result, the population has been forced to fend for itself.

The government advertises in its national and international propaganda that it continues to provide for the population, yet it hasn't done so for the best part of two decades. It continues to treat the [reality of starvation which has been going on for] over a generation as if it were a temporary, ancillary, and unwelcome phenomenon that will in some future scenario be eradicated when North Korea resumes its rightful place in the world as a "prosperous and strong nation".

In an absurd twist, the entrenched state mechanisms for oppression have created an atmosphere of mutual surveillance which demands that neighbour report on neighbour for any perceived disloyalty. This includes talking about hunger, because it implicates the state in failing to provide enough food. Everyone must live the same lie that all is well and that the government provides; to do otherwise results in forced labour in one of the unofficial but very real prison camps.

Professor Smith commented that it would be easy, when visiting Pyongyang, to be seduced by a superficial optimism that things have changed for the better. There have been some changes: apartment blocks and streets are illuminated at night; there is evidence of new shops and a few restaurants; and Pyongyang now has some traffic lights and an increasing number of cars to justify them. But all this conceals some harsh realities. North Korea is a country of extraordinary inequality, disparity, shortages, and acute poverty.

Today, the North is among the world's poorest nations and the South is among the richest. It is easy to forget that 40 years ago North Korea's Gross Domestic Product was twice that of the South. Along with its diplomatic relations, the country's economy and institutions have been allowed to become frozen in a time warp. What was a developed nation has become a severely underdeveloped nation.

Famine, a series of natural disasters, and the total collapse of the Soviet economies (once the DPRK's primary market) have all conspired to grind this country into abject poverty. As things stand, the situation is precarious.

Senior DPRK officials have told me that the average citizen receives only a meagre 350–400 grams of rice each day, well short of even the regime's sparse target of 600 grams. The truth is that many see no rice at all, subsisting instead on husky corn meal. I have also been told by DPRK escapees that in the north of the country there are no elderly people to be seen – they have all died.

David Austin, the North Korea programme director of Mercy Corps, said his charity has found pockets "throughout the country" where people "are starving to death". Austin confirmed that reports of desperate people eating bark, nettles, and insects to survive are true. He explained the grave implications of prolonged malnutrition: "The [people] haven't had enough food or drink dirty water from a flood, or for whatever reason, they get a cold and they are [too] weak from their malnutrition that they can't fight just a normal shock."

He described how North Koreans he had interviewed told him that all their household income had been spent on food and that "every single person knew the exact date of when they last had protein. People are emotionally fully engaged with their food and their nutrition. Their whole mindset is about food."[42]

Hazel Smith would strongly agree. Giving evidence to my parliamentary group, she warned us that "the under-20s have

---

42. *New York Times*, 24 October 2011.

never seen anything other than hunger. If food doesn't go in, there will be another famine, and soon."

The World Health Organization (WHO) reports fatality rates for children at 93 out of every 1,000, while the death rate among infants was cited as 23 out of every 1,000. Malnourished mothers are unable to maintain exclusive breast-feeding and, as infant formula is not produced in the country and no suitable alternative is available, babies simply die or become victims of chronic malnutrition. More than 37 per cent of six-year-olds in North Korea are said to be chronically malnourished.

The World Food Programme (WFP) reports rampant malnutrition and stunted growth in children. Stunted growth has already led – in an incredible and tragic illustration – to the minimum height requirement for entry into the North Korean army being reduced from 140 centimetres to 130 centimetres.

On average, boys in North Korea are 13 centimetres shorter than their South Korean counterparts and weigh 11 kilograms less. Malnutrition not only leads to physical weakness, it also leads to intellectual impairment. It leads to a frail population and makes the people especially vulnerable to disease.

More than a decade after the Arduous March, nothing has changed and the situation remains perilous. On 12 November 2012, the WFP issued a Special Report, warning that North Korea would suffer a shortfall of 507,000 tonnes of food in the growing year 2012–13. This represents one quarter of the total food needed to provide the basic requirements for the population. This leaves many millions of North Koreans facing acute food shortages, and the WFP reports that chronic "under-nutrition" remains a significant problem in all areas of the country.[43]

In January 2013, a number of newspapers printed harrowing reports of starving people exhuming and eating corpses and of

43. UN and WFP, *Special Report – FAO/WFP Crop and Food Security Assessment Mission to the Democratic People's Republic of Korea*, 12 November 2012.

hunger-maddened parents killing and eating their children.[44]

The environment is not making the situation any easier; 2012 saw the worst drought in a century. Most of the country's salt pans were destroyed in floods in the autumn of 2012 and the population was bracing itself for salt shortages and a hike in prices. The Director of Asia Press said in September 2012 that a combination of drought, flooding, and typhoons "coupled with the indifference of the authorities has led to the situation becoming very serious". The crime rate has increased, as people steal to feed their families and themselves. Though climate factors are significant, the greater part of the problem is that North Korea is a failing state without the means to feed its people.

I have seen this failure with my own eyes. In 2010, when Baroness Cox and I held talks with DPRK officials in Pyongyang, it was never long before food and crop failure were mentioned. That year, the cabbage crop had failed, meaning a scarcity of the *kim-chi* staple which sustains Korean families during the harsh winters.

At Sariwon, 40 kilometres from Pyongyang, Caroline Cox and I visited a co-operative farm and saw agricultural workers bringing in the last of a paltry harvest. Around the fields were signs and loudspeakers urging the workers to redouble their efforts. But without improved technology, different methods of agriculture, enhanced yields of crops, and pooling resources with the South, it is hard to see what more the workers can reasonably be expected to do.

In 2011, my colleague Baroness (Valerie) Amos, the United Nations' humanitarian chief, visited the DPRK and addressed my parliamentary committee on her return. She told us that the situation in North Korea has been "getting worse year on year"

---

44. "North Korean cannibalism fears amid claims starving people forced to desperate measures" by Rob Williams, *The Independent*, 28 January 2013.

and that North Korea runs short of food by about 1 million tonnes every year.

In her view, North Koreans urgently need outside aid to fight "terrible levels of malnutrition", especially among children. Unusually, the DPRK invited journalists in to see the level of malnourishment. Lady Amos told me that around "6 million North Koreans urgently need food aid, but the outside world is not giving enough. We need to remember the most vulnerable people in North Korea are victims of a situation over which they have no control. They are suffering through no fault of their own."

They are suffering for two straightforward reasons: North Korea *cannot* feed its people and the international community *will not* – and the North Korean people are paying the price. Member states of the international community – including the US and South Korea – have purposefully withheld food from the North Korean people in an effort to subdue the DPRK regime. In negotiating with the DPRK regime, the US and South Korea (among others) have made the mistake of linking the provision of food to other more inflammatory issues, such as North Korea's nuclear programme, missile development, and defence. Because of the regime's inevitable provocations, the North Korean population can no longer receive the lifeline of international food aid.

It is true that North Korea has scandalously used at least 30 per cent of its GDP on armaments and in developing nuclear weapons – resources that should have been used to develop the country's economy and agriculture. The country is being punished and the sanctions are "working" in that the vital supply of rice and other staples has been cut off.

Mauro Garofalo, spokesman for the Italian Catholic charity Community of Sant'Egidio, visited North Korea and reported that the "population lacks almost everything: first of all more and more nutritive food. But we could also see that they need detergents, disinfectants, drugs, and medical devices. Political considerations notwithstanding, the country's productive system has been severely put to the test by the US and UN embargoes, especially as a consequence of fuel scarcity."

In April 2012 an American food and aid programme – worth £126 million – was scrapped after the fiasco of North Korea's botched attempt to launch a satellite. The real victims of this failure of politics and diplomacy were the malnourished and starving children of North Korea – not the regime. The international community was well aware that the DPRK would attempt to launch a satellite and it should have thought twice before linking food aid to this. The consequence is an entire generation stunted both physically and developmentally.

Every political leader from Washington to Pyongyang, from London to Seoul, should be required to watch the grim footage released by the UN Food Programme, which shows health workers in western South Hwangae Province pulling on the loose skin of a crying child's belly. The promised aid included corn-soy porridge with vegetable oil, which was to be specially reserved for children and pregnant women.

America says that it is the North Koreans who, by their actions, are holding their own people hostage. North Korea says it shows America can't be trusted. What it does show – and what has been warned against over and over again – is that using food relief like a pawn in a deadly game of chess always ends badly. Over the years this has been a recurring pattern.

It has been almost 20 years since the terrible famines of the mid-1990s and the North Korean government still has not amended its behaviour in response to the withholding of food. The ordinary people have suffered and nothing has changed. Other forms of leverage must be used to effect change in the priorities of the DPRK regime. The international community needs to think very carefully about the morality, the appalling misery and poverty, and the long-term consequences of attempting to force North Korea into submission through the denial of food.

We must surely draw a distinction between a regime and its ideology on the one hand and the people on the other. Food must never be used as a weapon of war.

When at the State Department in Washington in 2012, I raised this directly with Ambassador Robert King, who was appointed by Barack Obama in 2009 as his Special Envoy for North Korean Human Rights Issues. He patiently explained that the US could do nothing more until after the US and South Korean elections later that year. The politics just didn't allow it.

It is an appalling tragedy when people become the victims of political stand-offs. Not wanting to look weak in the eyes of your electorate – whether in the United States or the Republic of Korea – can come at the cost of children losing their lives. A leader may look strong but only at the expense of someone else becoming weak, and such leaders lose their consciences in the effort to save face.

Whether or not the US or South Korean political interests choose to acknowledge it, the fact is that the people of North Korea are starving. Mercy Corps and four other US-based relief agencies operating in North Korea have accused Washington of ignoring their repeated warnings of an impending famine. David Austin claimed that it was "all wrapped in a political process" and that State Department officials had told him "It's an election year" when asked about Washington's unofficial policy in 2012.

What the State Department officials meant was that the votes of 2 million ethnically Korean Americans who live in the United States must be won, and politicians, in a tight contest, aim to do this by looking like tough leaders. The indirect consequence of chasing votes with hard-line rhetoric in one country is the starvation of the people of another. Although both Washington and Seoul deny linking food and humanitarian aid to political issues, the reality is entirely obvious.

By total contrast, another Democratic president was unequivocal on the subject. Jimmy Carter could not have been clearer when, in 2011, he said, "One of the most important human rights is to have food to eat, and for South Korea and the United States and others to withhold food aid to the North Korean people is really a human rights violation."[45]

To continue the policy of withholding food aid is unwarranted. And it was a mistake to link the provision of food to other issues, such as the attempted missile launches of 2012 or the repatriation of the remains of missing Americans lost during the Korean War. It means that when the North Korean regime breaks its word on such issues, the countries providing aid must suffer a major loss of face or allow ordinary Koreans to starve to death. This linkage brings no political benefit but risks the malnutrition and mass starvation of the population of North Korea.

South Korea's decision to withhold food aid, supported by the Obama Administration, has inevitably put innocent lives at risk while doing nothing to bring about the end of the conflict between North and South. You can't starve people into submission and you shouldn't try. The theory has been tried and it has proved an utter failure – North Korea has not "given in" because of food shortages.

I can only hope that a change in Seoul's Blue House and a more progressive course taken by President Obama in his second term will see the policy of using food as a weapon of war dropped for good. In the case of North Korea, the use of

45. Glyn Ford, "EU breaks the lock on hungry North Koreans", *The Japan Times*, 26 July 2011.

this weapon has done no apparent damage to the regime but the collateral damage to the civilian population has been sustained and devastating.

In the House of Lords, I argued that, whatever our dislike of a country's ideology or policies, we should never use food as a weapon of war, citing the dreadful impact of it on ordinary people, especially children.

Replying for the British government, Baroness (Lindsay) Northover said:

> *The noble Lord is right to say that there is a very high level of malnutrition across the world, which has a terrible impact upon the health of children. That is why the government have focused very much on trying to ensure that this issue is addressed… It is extremely important that we ensure that food – and support for the ability of people to feed themselves – is available worldwide, whatever the regime.*[46]

There are a few glimmers of hope. In August 2012, in Beijing, Chinese premier Wen Jiabao received a high-level delegation from the DPRK led by Jang Sung-taek, the uncle of Kim Jong-un. They met to discuss trade and economic ties. The very fact of their meeting was a subtle recognition by the isolationist DPRK that *Juche* is not and has not been enough for North Korea. Its leaders are not fools and are well aware that you can hardly claim to be self-reliant when your ambassadors must ask for food aid.

The previous North Korean Ambassador in London, Ja Song-nam, asked me to arrange meetings with agencies such as Christian Aid – and I did so, although many charities and non-

---

46. Baroness Lindsay Northover, Government Spokesperson in the House of Lords on International Development, replying to a question asked at the Food Security Summit, 25 July 2012, 11.30 a.m.

governmental organizations are reluctant to become involved because food has become the latest weapon of war.

Asking for help is an important step towards recovery, and people and organizations are responding. In May 2012 two organizations – Sant'Egidio and Caritas Korea – delivered 25 tonnes of food aid to the DPRK. This was done at the request of Han Tae-song, North Korea's former Ambassador to Rome. The consignment of rice, beans, sugar, and oil was distributed between two institutions for elderly people and one orphanage in a district about 100 kilometres south of Pyongyang.

These are small signs and acts which – though very important – cannot hope to help anything but a small proportion of the malnourished population of North Korea. Those interested in British history will know stories of a famine that claimed the lives of a million people, and how the failure of England to respond to the Great Starvation in Ireland's moment of need poisoned British–Irish relations for generations. We must learn from our own history and do all that we can to prevent it being repeated.

The continued denial of food aid cannot be morally justified. Food must never be used as a weapon of war.

CHAPTER 13

Building a Peace Process That Works

In the heart of Pyongyang, on the banks of the city's Taedong River, opposite Kim Il-sung Square, stands the Juche Tower. Completed in 1982 to celebrate Kim Il-sung's 70th birthday, the tower stands at 170 metres, marginally taller than the Washington Monument on which it appears to be modelled.

Like the country as a whole, the Juche Tower is in need of urgent repair.

In 2010, while making my third visit to North Korea, I was taken to see the tower. My embarrassed guide explained that we could not ascend it or even go near it because debris was falling from within onto the lift mechanism. The situation, he explained, was very dangerous, and it seemed an appropriately graphic metaphor for both North Korea's economy and the state's unstable foreign policy.

Everything had the scent of decay – but change was also in the air.

The Soviet model is discredited; its powerful neighbour, China, is in the throes of a liberalizing revolution, and North Korea knows that self-reliance will not be enough. Senior officials, including the Speaker of their Assembly, Choe Tae-bok, insisted to me that over the next two years the new priorities are "prosperity and dignity" with the creation of a "unified, denuclearized Korea" as their first objective. The West should listen carefully and respond appropriately; the alternative doesn't bear thinking about.

A necessary precondition of reunification is signing a peace treaty and formally ending the war. For nearly 60 years, the unstable ceasefire meant the US had no diplomatic presence in the DPRK. Now that the North Korean regime has declared the ceasefire dissolved,[47] the forging of new diplomatic ties and opening up of dialogues are even less likely than before. Ending the war could not be more urgent – to end the 60-year trauma and bring closure to the Korean peoples.

The human consequences of the Korean War still reverberate today in many tragic circumstances, none more so than the plight of Korean War Abductees. In November 2012 I encountered two representatives of families divided by that war. What struck me was that the pain of separation was still quite evident – even after the passage of so much time.

Lee Mi-il's father, Lee Seong-hwan, was one of an estimated 100,000 people who were abducted by the North Koreans during the course of hostilities and who have never been allowed to return to their families.

Mr Lee and his family had been trapped in their apartment after the North Koreans captured Seoul and blew up the Han River bridge. On 4 September 1950 a North Korean major came for Mr Lee, accused him of giving money to those fighting the Communists, and took him away. His wife, who was heavily pregnant with their second child, and is now in her nineties, never saw him again or heard any news about his fate.

She has spent a lifetime waiting for him to return.

Her daughter told me, "My mother says she has given up hope of seeing him before she dies, but I know she still has hope in her heart." She added, "I have promised that I will not stop my journey to find him until the end of time."

47. BBC News, *North Korea ends peace pacts with the South*,
www.bbc.co.uk/news/world-asia-21709917, 8 March 2013

Mr Lee's story, and that of his wife and daughter, is one of several testimonies contained in a short book with the well-chosen title *Ongoing Tragedy.*

The day after my meeting with Mr Lee's daughter, I encountered Hwang In-cheol. His father, Hwang Won, was abducted 16 years after the Korean War ceasefire in December 1969. His father worked as a programme director at Munhwa Broadcasting Corporation (MBC) and was travelling on an internal Korean Airlines flight from Gangneung to Seoul. North Koreans hijacked the plane and took the passengers hostage. Thirty-nine of them were repatriated 66 days later but another 11 were never returned, Hwang's father among them.

The International Red Cross tried to open lines of contact but North Korea simply said it was impossible to say whether the abductees were alive or not. Then in 2011 Pyongyang claimed that the abductees were there of their own free will. An escapee has confirmed that he has seen Hwang's father alive. Hwang has tried to get his own government in Seoul to raise his father's case but says they have failed to do so – and, although he has written to the North Korean authorities on three occasions, he has had no reply. The last time he saw his father he was just two years of age.

These people must be allowed home. Without such closure, the bitterest legacy will continue through the generations and the pain of the last 60 years will live on. If abductees are no longer alive, as much information as possible must be collected so that loved ones may put the questions to rest and find some solace. If North Korea ever wants to send a signal that it understands the pain of human separation, it should respond to Mr Hwang's requests and it should allow Mrs Lee to end her days knowing what happened to her husband.

The first step towards achieving this – and countless other objectives – is peace. But how do we get there?

A new peace conference could be held in Beijing, jointly convened by a neutral nation and a combatant – Switzerland and the UK, perhaps. In such a context, North and South Korea could formally end the war and conclude a peace treaty. This would change everything, not least of all by breathing new life into the Six-Party Talks on denuclearization. To get here, a lot of groundwork must be done – but it could begin tomorrow if there were enough political courage in the leadership of South Korea and the USA.

These two nations could cancel their annual regattas of the most heavily armed and largest vessels in the American and South Korean navies. In addition, provocative exercises along the 38th Parallel by US and South Korean troops could be scaled back. These unnecessary and highly provocative displays do little to convince North Korea that its hated "enemies" have peaceful intentions.

Naturally, the US and South Korea would probably respond by saying that a country that has been testing nuclear weapons and which has a standing army of over a million men must be deterred by regular displays of force.

Both attitudes point to escalation and it will take courage to step back from this showdown. This is the Korean version of the Cold War: two sides relying on MAD (mutually assured destruction) and chest-thumping to keep the other at bay. If the war ever became "hot", the loss of life would be colossal. Foreign allies of both states would be drawn in to the war but undoubtedly the vast majority of lives lost would be Korean, simply because the conflict would be played out on the peninsula.

Unless there is change, North and South Korea will remain a threat to one another, waiting for a "Sarajevo moment" to occur.

In 1914, the Bosnian Serb Gavrilo Princip went to Sarajevo on the business of the secretive Black Hand group. The Black Hand's objectives were to free the south-Slav provinces from the rule of the occupying Austro-Hungarian Empire and to create a Greater Serbia. The group's method was to use the death of Archduke Franz Ferdinand of Austria as a catalyst for mobilizing a revolution. As the world knows, it sparked more than a revolution: a war in which over 16 million people died and 20 million were wounded.

There is even credible evidence that suggests that the Black Hand was manipulated into precipitating war by high-ranking members of the Serbian military intelligence. With this in mind, it is worth considering the motivation behind events such as the 2010 sinking of the *Cheonan* and the shelling of Yeonpyeong Island. Were these attacks authorized by the North Korean political leadership or by others with the encouragement of factions within the North Korean military? Either way, they were extraordinarily dangerous moments which, beyond the personal tragedy of the deceased servicemen, had the capacity to become Sarajevo moments and drag the peninsula, the region, and perhaps the world into a devastating war.

There is also the residual danger that the desperation of the northern regime – faced again by widespread famine and starvation and a failure to introduce Chinese-style economic reforms – might consider a desperate "last fling of the dice" and invade the South, all done under the reliable old pretext of liberating their countrymen from Western imperialist oppression.

To avoid such scenarios we need a more reasoned and nuanced approach than mutually assured destruction.

The way forward is a readoption of a modified Sunshine Policy, similar to the original which President Lee so regrettably abandoned. The starting assumptions would be threefold: first, that force will always be met by equal force and both sides will categorically renounce territorial ambitions; second, the peace process would aim to achieve, in the long term, the complete denuclearization of the peninsula; and, third, all progress would point to the reunification of Korea.

Creating the necessary traction to reach such a conclusion will require a patient "small-steps" strategy and a better understanding of North Korea. Too often Western strategists have equated North Korea with the former Soviet bloc and assumed that the DPRK will behave as other Communist countries have behaved. North Korea is not going to become tomorrow's Poland, Hungary, or Romania.

Western thinking has also neglected the experience of Korea at the hands of the Japanese occupiers. Japan must acknowledge its war crimes if healing is to begin. This would erode the power of the DPRK's xenophobic and inflammatory rhetoric and undermine the regime's promotion of itself as a benevolent protector of the people against the corrupt and brutal foreigner.

There are further assumptions about North Korea which need to be re-examined. Unlike its Soviet allies, the DPRK never saw itself as international. It is difficult to imagine the North Korean leadership enthusiastically singing the Communist "Internationale", the rallying song for Communists across the globe:

> *Let the armies go on strike… and break ranks.*
> *If they insist, these cannibals,*
> *on making heroes of us,*
> *they will know soon that our bullets*
> *are for our own generals.*
> *This is the final struggle;*
> *let us group together, and tomorrow*
> *the "Internationale"*
> *will be the human race.*

It will not have been lost on the North Korean leadership that the same anthem was sung with suitable irony by the East German protesters arrested by the state in 1989 and the students and workers at China's Tiananmen Square protests also of 1989, who sang with heavy emphasis the refrain that "the 'Internationale' will win our human rights".

The DPRK's leaders will perhaps be relieved that, unlike the Soviets, they have never emphasized the idea of international brotherhood or worldwide revolution, but by the same token the West should acknowledge that the DPRK has not harboured or promoted serious territorial ambitions beyond the Korean peninsula.

The North Korean leaders know that the US has no more intention of invading North Korea than it had of invading Albania or Romania – but the leadership also knows that state propaganda has led the people to believe that the DPRK government's primary function is to keep America at bay. The fiction of an American aggressor must therefore continue. North Korea has become trapped by its own rhetoric but it also faces the critical need to re-engage with the world if it is to survive.

English essayist William Hazlitt (1778–1830) understood the nature of deception when he said, "In order that the deception may succeed it must be habitual and uninterrupted." The DPRK does this very well. During my first visit to North Korea in 2003, I was struck by the never-ending invective against the US which our guides and minders had been schooled into offering as an explanation for any failing in the regime.

A 2012 Associated Press report further underlined the importance of changing both the language and the climate to enable proper dialogue to occur. The report described posters on the walls of DPRK kindergarten classrooms, showing "bright-eyed children brandishing rifles and bayonets" and attacking a wounded American soldier.

The posters were headed by anti-American slogans, such as "We love playing military games knocking down the American bastards". Another poster, proclaiming the call to arms "Let's wipe out the US imperialists", showed the image of an American with a noose around his neck.

The journalist went on to describe how visitors to the school saw toy pistols, rifles, and tanks on classroom shelves. The school's head teacher, Yun Song-sil, even exhibited a dummy of an American soldier, "with a beaked nose and straw-coloured hair". The children charge the dummy in mock-bayonet drills and beat it with batons. Yun Song-sil said this "favourite playground game" is the way in which the "children learn from an early age about the American bastards".

The American bogeyman is the primary culprit for every shortcoming, with South Korea's jealous puppet government a close second. Any reconciliation process would quickly fail that first did not dismantle these DPRK myths, which have been ingrained in generation after generation.

The most straightforward way of dismantling this obstacle to understanding is to replace the face of the bogeyman with real human faces. Of course, it would be unwise to send American GIs into North Korea to meet primary-school children – but the strategy of bringing ordinary people face to face where they can discover each other's humanity can work and has worked in similar situations.

This gentle tactic helped to end the Cold War. Termed "Confidence-Building Measures", or CBMs, the method brought colourful human faces out from behind the monochrome uniforms of war and helped thaw Europe's frozen military relationships. It blazed a trail along which many other peace-building measures could follow.

The 1975 Helsinki Final Act of the Conference on Security and Co-operation in Europe stated that CBMs would "contribute to reducing the dangers of armed conflict and of misunderstanding or miscalculation of military activities which could give rise to apprehension, particularly in a situation where states lack clear and timely information". The United Nations has since extended the definition to include non-military measures and to cover "actions taken to reduce or eliminate the causes of mistrust, fear, tension and hostility amongst modern states".

In short, Confidence-Building Measures do what the name suggests – they build confidence and break down distrust. Typically, CBMs are used to eliminate security concerns, to minimize the possibility of unintended war, and to introduce disarmament and weapons control. Although they can be legally binding, CBMs tend to be more flexible, remaining politically rather than legally binding.

It is difficult to predict the success of CBMs with the North Korean regime because of the deeply entrenched militaristic *Songun* policy. However, the very fact that the DPRK regime is so proud of its military capabilities might be the thing that opens the door to a discussion about joint exercises or other forms of military co-operation.

A less controversial or risky start may be made by the non-military equivalent of CBMs: the Confidence-Enhancing Measures. CEMs are civilian measures that tend to be less rigidly defined than the military CBMs and can pose no conceivable threat to security or state sovereignty. In the case of North Korea, CEMs may find a way through the high walls of the isolationist DPRK more easily.

CEMs can include anything from activities such as joint study groups to shared representation at international sporting events – just as the Republic of Ireland and Northern Ireland play together in international Rugby Union tournaments. In the Korean situation, a joint North–South team at the 2012 London

Olympics would have increased their haul of medals to 34, with 17 gold medals, and resulted in an even more impressive lead over Germany and France.

The scope for small steps and enhancing confidence-building is wide, and every effort adds more real human faces to counterbalance the bogeymen of North Korean propaganda. There is already a precedent for a host of complementary CEMs to be rolled out on the Korean peninsula.

The 1991 Basic Agreement between Kim Jong-il's North and Roh's South Korea was a landmark in North–South relations because it called for reconciliation and co-operation by establishing four joint commissions. These commissions focused on South–North reconciliation, South–North military affairs, South–North economic exchanges and co-operation, and South–North social and cultural exchange.

Sadly, the enormous potential for co-operation was never realized. Plans made in the fields of trade, science, technology, education, literature, and travel were never fully implemented owing to the inevitable rounds of provocation, outrage, and isolation that North Korea has found so rewarding. Efforts were made to pursue these plans via the Sunshine Policy, but it was done without accompanying commitments to security-related Confidence-Building Measures and the plans achieved far less than was hoped.

Nevertheless, even stalled or failed initiatives – everything from Mount Kumgang tourism to family exchanges to economic projects such as the joint Kaesŏng Industrial Park – could be re-energized and melt the frosty relations. Though the states may try to remain faceless, the unfiltered interactions of ordinary citizens from both countries can totally undermine their efforts.

If the new round of Sunshine-style engagement is to succeed, such face-to-face interactions must take place within a wider process which ensures that humanitarian crimes, past and present, are acknowledged and dealt with. The old wounds of war and the more recent wounds of dictatorship must be healed if northern and southern states are to meet with any real hope of reunion.

The best model we have for such a process comes from the dismantling of the wider Cold War, when a divided world met in Dipoli, Helsinki, and succeeded in thawing the Cold War tensions while simultaneously protecting the humanitarian rights of the populations of the Communist bloc. So that the world can avoid a nuclear-powered Sarajevo moment and the two Korean states can work towards a meaningful reunion, what we need is another Helsinki, this time with a Korean face.

CHAPTER 14

Helsinki with a Korean Face:
Human Rights and Security

In 2005 I organized a visit to North Korea by Field Marshal General the Lord Guthrie of Craigiebank, formerly Chief of the Defence Staff under Prime Ministers John Major and Tony Blair. He was accompanied by Brigadier Tom Ogilvie-Graham, who had worked with the Iraq survey group, and James Mawdsley, the Christian human rights activist who had spent more than a year in Burmese prisons, where he had experienced the hard reality of oppression.

General Guthrie's illustrious military credentials paved the way for an unprecedented meeting with DPRK army officers, including General Kim Sang-ik, deputy minister of the People's Armed Forces.

The meeting did not go smoothly.

As expected, our DPRK hosts fed General Guthrie the predictable lines about how "it is all down to the USA to drop their hostile policy", and that "human rights in North Korea cannot easily be measured by a Western yardstick". Most insulting of all was their insistence that "the first human right is national sovereignty, without which life has no meaning. So our government provides the people with the right to exist."

General Guthrie responded coolly but firmly, stating, "I am shocked when you say human rights is about the right to exist. It is about much more than that. It is about dignity. It is about fairness. It is about freedom of choice." But at least the ice had been broken – perhaps demonstrating the accuracy of

Churchill's remark at a White House luncheon in 1954 that "to jaw-jaw is always better than to war-war".

Throughout the Cold War, the West countered Soviet aggression with formidable defences. At the same time Margaret Thatcher and Ronald Reagan encouraged economic and political reform and – critically – they elevated the discourse on human rights through the Helsinki Process. On the Korean peninsula, as I have already stated, we need what I have called Helsinki with a Korean face.

Timothy Sowula, who works for the British Council in London, described the signing of the 1975 Helsinki Accords as creating a "chink in the armour of state socialism" which led directly to the "bursting illumination"[48] of 1989 when the Berlin Wall was torn down. Crucial to this process, Mr Sowula recognized, was Article 7 of the Accords, which guaranteed "the freedoms of thought, speech, conscience, religion and faith of all citizens of the signatory states".

US President Ronald Regan talked the language of Helsinki on 12 June 1987, just two years before the fall of the Berlin Wall, when he said:

> *We welcome change and openness; for we believe that freedom and security go together, that the advance of human liberty can only strengthen the cause of world peace. There is one sign the Soviets can make that would be unmistakable, that would advance dramatically the cause of freedom and peace. General Secretary Gorbachev, if you seek peace, if you seek prosperity for the Soviet Union and eastern Europe, if you seek liberalization, come here to this gate. Mr. Gorbachev, open this gate. Mr. Gorbachev, tear down this wall!*

---

48. Timothy Sowula, www.opendemocracy.net, 1 August 2005.

The Helsinki Final Act, Helsinki Accords, and Helsinki Declaration are three names for one thing: the final act of the Conference on Security and Co-operation in Europe. The conference was held in Helsinki, Finland, during July and August of 1975 when 35 states signed a declaration to improve the relations between the Communist bloc and the West. It sent a signal that reached over the Iron Curtain and carried a message that division and oppression would end all across Eastern Europe.

Likewise, the principal objective of Helsinki with a Korean face must be the dismantling of a wall that separates Koreans, just as in 1989 the wall that separated German from German and European from European was pulled down for good. Central to this must be the use of "soft power with a hard-headedness", focusing on healing the past and creating a future.

But what to do, exactly? Baroness Cox and I laid out specific recommendations in our report, "Finding a Way Forward", in which we said that a Helsinki-style process should link security and human rights issues. We called for the formal ending of the Korean War, the creation of an American diplomatic presence in Pyongyang, and a sustained elevation of human rights concerns.

Lady Cox and I have quietly persisted with constructive, critical engagement. Year by year we have been building up a consensus around new forms of engagement.

In 2004, in Parliament, I told the House of Lords:

> *I believe that hard-headed, Helsinki-style engagement is worthwhile. The Helsinki Final Act 1975 linked foreign policy to basic human rights principles. That measure recognized that increasing the pressure for human rights, in combination with a firm policy of military containment, could act as the catalyst for change. The history of the DPRK*

> *suggests that mere threats will be counter-productive...*
> *However, the regime knows that the status quo is not an*
> *option. The DPRK now needs a face-saving exit strategy.*

Helsinki defeated the tyranny it faced and today the Helsinki spirit offers the most constructive way forward. And we who enjoy freedom should use it ceaselessly to shine a light on individual cases and situations.

South Korean human rights groups have been methodical in telling the stories of suffering and laying the truth bare: this needs to continue and ever more links should be made with parliamentarians around the world – as happened during the Helsinki Process. The European Union should provide resources to enable North Korean refugees and journalists to share their stories with a worldwide audience.

As mentioned in this book's introduction, making human rights a pivotal issue has also been advocated by the American North Korea expert David Hawk. His 2010 report, "Pursuing Peace While Advancing Rights: The Untried Approach to North Korea", concluded that Helsinki "is the approach that has yet to be tried in North Korea", but he also said that "for the last 20 years, the paradigm that has guided approaches to the DPRK [has required] that human rights concepts be kept off the table and that [we] affect a deaf, dumb, blind and mute posture toward the systematic, severe, and widespread human rights violations in the DPRK."

He continued: "[There is] an alternative that would pursue peace, engagement, and reconciliation in association with the promotion and protection of human rights: a fundamentally new and untried approach."

We must continue to push for this approach to be tried because, until we do, the human rights violations in the DPRK will go on unchallenged.

"Justice" in North Korea

Lady Cox and I made our third visit to North Korea in October 2010. During that visit we went to see the building that houses North Korea's Supreme Court. There we met a Senior Law Officer, with whom we discussed two key areas of concern.

First, as we were given a tour of the courtroom, it became evident that the defendant in a trial is already deemed guilty, as reflected in the structure of the courtroom, in which the defendant is placed in a small wooden enclosure, seated on a small, very uncomfortable stool, in contrast to the more comfortable chairs provided for others. The Senior Law Officer confirmed to us that the principle of "innocent until proven guilty" *does not apply* in the North Korean judicial system. "Most defendants are those whose crime has already been revealed, before indictment, by investigation by the police. When a person comes to court, we do not think of them as innocent," he said.

Furthermore, it appeared that the legal defence available for the defendant becomes actively involved in the process only once the "suspect" is brought to trial and all the relevant evidence against them has been prepared. We urged the DPRK authorities to make sure that the accused receives legal help before the trial.

North Korea has made some progress in the matter of criminal justice. Human rights groups have described as "positive" the changes made to the Criminal Code and Criminal Procedure Code in 2004 and 2005. Unfortunately, defectors' testimonies still suggest an inconsistency between the law and its application.

Such an inconsistency has dreadful implications for a country that still applies the death penalty. Exact numbers are unknown and difficult to verify, but this sentence is given to all sections of society – not just to members of the lowest classes and the powerless. For example, it was reported that former Finance Minister Pak Nam-gi was executed in March 2010, following the currency devaluation crisis. It is worth noting that on 7 October 2010 the European Parliament adopted a resolution to mark the World Day Against the Death Penalty, in which it specifically urged North Korea "to immediately and permanently stop public executions".

In our discussions with DPRK officials, we presented a list of countries that have abolished or strictly limited the use of the death penalty. Excluding China and South Korea, 9 out of 10 of North Korea's top donor countries prohibit the death penalty. Even countries such as Russia and Burma, while not officially abolishing the death penalty, can be considered abolitionist in practice because they have not executed anyone for 10 years and are believed to have a policy of not implementing the death penalty.

We also raised the ugly subject of torture and were pleased to hear that the DPRK Criminal Procedure Code bans evidence "acquired from the accused through repression or coercion". The DPRK Senior Law Officer told us that if "coercive measures" are found to have been used, the authorities investigate and those who have used such measures are prosecuted. These were fine sentiments, but cases of severe beatings by prison guards and interrogators since 2004 are widely documented.[49]

Beatings are only part of the picture. Testimonies by former prisoners suggest that sexual harassment, assault, and rape of female detainees is common, even though the government appears to criminalize rape.

We called on the DPRK representatives to answer many more challenging and uncomfortable questions. We reminded

---

49. See the Citizens' Alliance for North Korean Human Rights, Free the North Korean Gulag, and the Committee for Human Rights in North Korea.

them that Article 158 of their own constitution states that "court cases are heard in public and the accused is guaranteed the right of defence". The reality is often very different, however, as provisions allow police to "determine the length of sentence on the spot" and to send even a minor offender to the Kyo-yang-so "re-education" facility "without a trial". Such an enormous loophole in the criminal justice system is, unfortunately, included for a reason, and it is reported that even cases of defamation result in "re-education" without trial.

An overwhelming 96 per cent of defectors interviewed by the Korean Bar Association were given no explanation at the time of their arrest, and 90 per cent did not believe the investigation agency followed due procedure.

In the face of such facts, it is sad (yet unsurprising) that the DPRK authorities continue to deny the use of detention without trial or on-the-spot trials. Nevertheless, we shall continue to raise the subject as part of the "soft power with a hard-headedness" alluded to earlier.

"There are no prison camps"

We raised the subject of the prison camps, but the judicial authorities denied their existence. When we specifically named Camp 15 at Yodok, we were told that there were no prisons at all in Yodok. Such stories, the officials claimed, were fabrications made up by "criminals" with "sinister intentions", and should not be held up as prime examples. "Anyone who forsakes the motherland and goes to another country is a criminal wanting to justify themselves," an official told us.

When we presented the specific example of Shin Dong-hyok – who was born in Camp 14 in 1982, who saw his mother and brother publicly executed, and who was tortured many times including once by being roasted over a fire – we asked how he could be a criminal. We asked repeatedly whether we, or any foreigners, could visit the prisons and were told emphatically "No".

We will continue to ask. We will also pursue other human rights issues with the North Korean regime.

The DPRK Constitution sets the minimum working age at 16 years old, adding: "The State shall prohibit child labour under the stipulated working age." However, human rights organizations believe that children below the age of 16 are routinely treated as cheap labour by schools and teachers under the guise of various "campaigns", "projects", and "assignments". Furthermore, while desperate circumstances lead many children to resort to stealing in order to survive, incidents of theft are severely punished.

The Asian Centre for Human Rights (ACHR) reports cases of 11-year-old children being sent to forced labour camps for stealing electric wires, despite the DPRK's claim in a report in 1996 under the Convention on the Rights of the Child (CRC) that "institutions for reform through labour do not have juvenile inmates". When we queried these reports, officials in the DPRK denied detaining children as young as 11.

We urged the DPRK authorities to open up all detention and investigation facilities for regular and rigorous inspection by appropriate judicial inspectors and international monitors, including the UN Special Rapporteur on Human Rights in North Korea and the International Committee of the Red Cross (ICRC). We made it clear that we would be very happy to arrange a visit for a DPRK delegation to visit British prisons and courtrooms and meet with judicial and penal authorities in the UK.

We will continue to ask the questions until we receive genuine answers. This process could be eased by some non-military Confidence-Building Measures, such as meetings between judges and lawyers from the international community and the DPRK to "compare notes".

With international help, grounds for the use of on-site, on-the-spot trials could be clarified, and accused citizens granted access to legal defence and a clear explanation of their rights and the reason for their arrest. Judicial authorities could also be encouraged to develop the principle of "innocent until proven guilty".

We also offered the DPRK authorities the opportunity to meet former North Korean defectors now living in exile, such as Shin Dong-hyok, in a neutral location, so that they can hear first-hand the experiences of people who have fled the prison camps. Such CBEs would be painful but could begin the healing process.

Baroness Cox and I have needed hard heads to keep this dialogue going with the DPRK. We need a determined and co-ordinated Helsinki-style approach by European and other democratic governments and parliaments to open up these sorts of conversations on many more fronts. And we need restrained and targeted sanctions – the "soft power" – which will begin to open doors and save lives.

The previous strategy for dealing with North Korea – based on threats and counter-threats, blackmail, and tit-for-tat sanctions – is a proven failure and must be consigned to history.

The United States of America, which played a central role in the success of the original Helsinki Process, has failed to learn from its own achievements. In the Cold War, the US maintained an embassy in Moscow. This meant that the Siberian Seven – seven Pentecostal Christians fleeing brutal persecution – had somewhere to take refuge. Likewise, in China as recently as 2012, the US Embassy in Beijing was able to protect the brave blind human rights activist Chen Guangcheng as he staged a brave escape from a four-year jail term after challenging China's one-child policy. Chen and his family are now in the USA.

Despite this, it is disappointing to hear from senior Obama Administration officials that a diplomatic presence in

Pyongyang is unlikely "to happen any time soon". If America were to announce to the world a decision to open an embassy in North Korea – as a symbol of its values and belief in democracy, human rights, personal freedom, and liberty – it would be making a single-stroke statement that would shatter ice and deliver new hope. Such an announcement need not and should not be part of any larger bargain or require word-breaking negotiations. If it was right for America to be in the former Soviet Union – or in places such as Romania and Albania – then why not North Korea?

The small episodes involving embassies, which I have described, are very powerful stories of why holding nation states accountable for human rights is so important. The Siberian Seven and Chen Guangcheng put faces to the statistics that – even in large numbers – can numb us to the reality they attempt to describe.

The number of inmates in North Korean prisons is approximately 200,000. This is harder to brush away when we consider that every digit of that number is a man, a woman or a child with a unique face and their own story to tell. Embassies, as well as engaging with the state, can also remind us of the importance of human faces.

Britain, to its credit, has had an ambassador and embassy in Pyongyang since 2000 – and this has enhanced our ability to engage the country's leadership and to influence it towards a better future. Jim Hoare broke the ground by establishing the UK diplomatic mission and has been followed by exemplary ambassadors: John Everard, Peter Hughes, Karen Wolstenholme, and David Slinn. These diplomats have been widely admired for their thoughtful diplomacy, their decency, and their refusal to give up on finding a peaceful way forward.

It is often said that the North Korean regime has managed to exist behind a wall of secrecy; that it treats the international community with contempt by refusing to allow outside observers into the country. In the end the truth will out. First-hand witness accounts from North Korean defectors and escapees – such as those I have documented and those which have been archived by the NKDB – and increasing levels of communication with those who live there are a clue to the mass of evidence pointing towards egregious crimes against humanity in the DPRK. Just as the Soviet Union, under Mikhail Gorbachev (the grandson of a gulag survivor), ultimately banished the gulags to history, one day they will be consigned to history in North Korea too.

The "soft-power" approach of nurturing reform and democracy in North Korea while maintaining a focus on human rights must surely be the most effective way to proceed. We must try Helsinki with a Korean face.

There is a Korean proverb, *Karure tanbi* – May there be sweet rain in a drought – that refers to the cherished hope that something longed for may come about. Peace and reunification are certainly longed for, and we have the ability to bring them about.

CHAPTER 15

Why China Matters – Two Systems, One Country

I first visited mainland China 30 years ago. At the time of my visit, Shanghai was still affected by the excesses of the Cultural Revolution, and was trapped in a time warp.

I travelled there with the late David Atkinson MP[50] and we visited some of the underground churches that still operated in spite of state persecution. We were taken secretly to a spot where we could see the jailed Bishop of Shanghai, Bishop (later Cardinal) Kung, as he stood at a barred window looking out into the dusk. It was a sombre moment.

We visited an Anglican church which had been turned into workshops and squats – washing lines were strung between its windows. In the main square I recall the sensation of being a minority of one in a vast sea of people. Yet some of them began to tell me in enthusiastic tones how much they appreciated the BBC World Service broadcasts, which they had come to trust and which gave them a window on the world.

Although there was still a sense of fear and the anxiety that the country might revert to its Maoist past, there was a sense of excitement as if change was just around the corner.

Just two years earlier, in 1978, the reformist Deng Xiaoping had begun China's economic reform, which included the introduction of capitalist market principles. The reforms were implemented in two stages. First came the de-collectivization of

---

50. David Atkinson was the Conservative Member of Parliament for Bournemouth East from 1977 until 2005.

agriculture, the opening up of the country to foreign investment, and permission for businesses to be founded. Then, in the late 1980s and early 1990s, the state-privatized industry and price controls were "opened up" by deregulation, and trade and economic activity became a little more free. Between 1978 and 2010 unprecedented growth occurred. The economy increased by 9.5 per cent a year, finally faltering in 2012. China's economy is now second only to that of the United States.

North Korea could learn much from China's story and China could do much to help North Korea claim that story for its own.

China is an ancient civilization and home to a great people. In many ways, though, it is also a new country in the making and the jury remains out on whether its economic reforms will be matched by continuing political reform – alluded to by the incoming President Xi Jinping. One of the most interesting commentators to have written about the emerging China is Martin Jacques, whom I met in 2011 – but the story he tells suggests that North Korea needs to look south if it is to become a plural and free society as well as one with a prosperous economy.

For more than a decade, Jacques had been editor of *Marxism Today* and had transformed the magazine of the Communist Party of Great Britain from an obscure ideological organ of the Marxist Left into a broad platform for wide-ranging political and social debate. The magazine contributed to the public debate so much that it was even credited with coining the term "Thatcherism".

In 2012 he published *When China Rules the World: The End of the Western World and the Birth of a New Global Order*, his assessment of China's future role as the dominant global power. The title provides a useful summary of his thesis. My main reservation was that he was perhaps too willing to overlook the true nature of the Chinese political system as he dwelt on China's extraordinary growth, economic capacity, and cultural richness.

Taken to its logical end, brushing over humanitarian considerations in favour of economic success is something to be condemned, not celebrated, and I would like to have heard more from Jacques about the relationship between economic success and humanitarian outrage.

Jacques is well aware of stories such as that of Ai Weiwei, the celebrated Chinese artist and political activist who was incarcerated in Chinese jails for two months in 2012, and Chen Guangcheng, the blind civil and human rights activist mentioned in the previous chapter.

Neither Ai Weiwei nor Cheng Guangcheng would dismiss the importance of a healthy concern for human rights as being simply a way for the declining West to patronize the rising China. Jacques argued that there is no widespread desire for democracy or for the "enlightenment values" of the West. The dangerous extension of Jacques' argument would be to conclude that because the Communist state has created economic growth[51] this confers legitimacy on all the activities of that state.

I am certain Jacques would agree that during the 1930s the world's political Left made a catastrophic mistake in overlooking the enormities of Stalin's colossal abuses of human rights on the basis that he was a "successful" dictator. It was foolish to hope his drive for industrialization would relieve inequalities, and – as history has shown – he was not preferable to Hitler. Stalin famously remarked: "A single death is a tragedy; a million deaths is a statistic." Stalin, Hitler, and Mao sacrificed millions of individuals as they pursued a political dogma.

Whether the state is flourishing (like China) or decaying (like North Korea), commentators of all hues cannot afford to unhitch human rights concerns from economic performance

---

51. A Pew Poll indicated that over 91 per cent of Chinese people are satisfied with China's economic performance.

or any other measure of legitimacy. We must apply the same rigorous standard to both extremes.

China has operated the "one-child family" policy for some time now and the human cost has been horrifying because the three most lethal and dangerous words have become "It's a girl" – the title of a short movie whose premiere I hosted at Westminster in 2012. The killing of baby girls in China has led to there being 37 million more males than females, fuelling human trafficking and sexual slavery. Despite the fact that China is a truly great nation, it is important to offer severe criticism of the ideology that has led to such excesses.

What is incontestably true about Jacques' portrait of China is that, at a moment when our Western economies are in crisis and stagnating, China has continued to accelerate, albeit falteringly, of late.

In 1992 just 3.5 per cent of America's imports came from China; today it is 14.5 per cent. In Brazil it was 0.9 per cent while today it is 14 per cent. In the UK it has gone from virtually nothing in 1990 to 6 per cent of our imports today. And 20 per cent of Australia's imports come from China, while its two-way trade with its near neighbours – Taiwan, Singapore, and even Japan – soars. Over the next five years we will see the Chinese currency, the renminbi (RNB) – "the people's currency" – increasingly challenge the mighty US dollar.

China is moving into markets in every corner of the globe – particularly in Africa – and Jacques rightly says that "the developing world and China are umbilically linked". The rise of China and the rise of the developing world will march hand in hand.

The parallels for China's present and North Korea's future are very clear. China's economic engagement with the world creates opportunities for cultural change. In Africa, Chinese self-interest will also have to come to terms with democratic legitimacy and the rights of sovereign nations. And the fact that Chinese workers are travelling more and becoming exposed to democracy, free speech, religious freedom, and human rights will certainly affect the way they see themselves in relationship to their own state. China may be moving into Africa to secure much-needed natural resources, but it will bring home more than it bargained for in the face-to-face osmosis of cultural exchange.

China will not be transformed beyond all recognition by such exposure – but there will be significant shifts. Jacques rightly contends that Confucianism still shapes what is the very best of China today, but here he overlooks one important point: he says nothing about the rise of Christianity in China. By many calculations forecasting growth, China is set to become the nation in the world with the largest number of Christians.

North Korea, which has long demonized Christianity as a tool of the American imperialist, would be terrified if such a trend showed up in its measurements. However, for China, Christians may hold the key to keeping this "civilization state" together.

With over a billion citizens, 800 million of whom earn less than $2 a day, China's economic progress could be threatened by either of two things: the US pulling up the drawbridge to cheap Chinese imports or internal dissent threatening China's cohesion. With the exponential growth of Christianity in the country, China needs to decide what it is going to do with the question of religious freedom. The right or wrong decision on this subject could either protect or destroy China's social and political cohesion.

Like Korea, China should recall its positive experience with Christian missionaries such as Matteo Ricci as it works out its attitude to religious belief.

The imprisonment of Chinese Christians – including Protestant house-church leaders, underground Catholic bishops and the recent house arrest of Shanghai's brave Bishop Ma – has increasingly alienated men and women who would otherwise be loyal citizens, thus threatening the country's cohesion. Last year, around two dozen pastors and elders were among 160 people arrested at Beijing's 1,000-strong Shouwang Church.

Such actions alienate America and the nations of Europe, where human rights considerations help shape political and economic policies. Human rights could be the very issue that leads to Chinese isolation from the massive American market for its products.

And Christians in China are not an obscure minority. According to Yu Jianrong, a professor at the Chinese Academy of Social Sciences Rural Development Institute, there are between 45 and 60 million Protestant house-church Christians, with a further 18 to 30 million people attending government-approved churches. This is a significant proportion of the population.

Positive change may come to China if it decides to allow its people the religious freedom they deserve. Many Chinese people who have no faith tell me that, without religious values, China is in danger of becoming a nation of unbridled capitalism, where market forces and vast discrepancies between the poorest and the richest will create huge social tensions. Without the culture of giving and generosity inspired by religious values, China will be mired in corruption, lawlessness, and division. Its very cohesion will be threatened.

China could thus be held together or broken by its attitude to Christians. And this has great relevance to and provides lessons for North Korea today. The DPRK has oppressed its own people in every imaginable way and, as a direct consequence, the country is in a deplorable state. By ensuring human rights and allowing religious freedom, the North Korean leadership might find a valuable ally in its own people as it works to build its long-held dream of "a strong and prosperous nation".

China and Korea represent great civilizations and cultures and are possessed of wonderful people whom I have come to greatly admire. What China did in the mid-1970s and what North Korea now has to do is create political and economic systems worthy of their people.

Thirty years ago Shanghai and Pyongyang were similar cities. Pyongyang may yet catch up, with the right reforms to encourage freedom and real growth. Although 30 years have passed since North Korea took a different path from China, the opportunities to create prosperity and peace are still there.

Two systems, one country

If the DPRK leadership could ever be brought to the table to discuss peace and reunification, it would be done with the aid of one of their oldest ideological allies – China. And China can also provide an intriguing model for how North and South Korea could work towards a realistic future of reunification. China's sheer size makes it far more diverse and flexible than the West often gives it credit for and, though we may like to think of it in simplistic terms as a huge red state, the existence of Hong Kong, with its two systems in one country, reminds us that it is anything but simplistic.

Once at the negotiating table, the North Korean regime would be hard-pressed to articulate a legitimate rejection of why two systems in one country could work. Hong Kong is one of China's most prosperous and socially progressive cities.

Hong Kong is a vibrant and functioning demonstration of how two separate societies can integrate and, with time, become one. It is the nearest example, both geographically and culturally, to North and South Korea, and Hong Kong also shows how Communist ideology can get along with liberal, democratic, and regulated capitalism to the benefit of all. One only has to visit other major Chinese cities such as Shanghai to see which "side" is dominating the cultural exchange.

As China's partner in Hong Kong, Britain would be well placed to assist, advise, and encourage this stage of the negotiation. The novel constitutional arrangements devised by Deng Xiaoping and Geoffrey Howe (now Lord Howe) for Hong Kong – two systems in one country – would be the preliminary way to take the project forward.

The Helsinki-style engagement could then move forward with confidence towards a "two-systems" solution. For this to work, there would need to be objectives that both parts of the single state would need to have as their aim. It would have to become a country where respect for human dignity and basic rights was contained in both systems. If a reunited Korea is to be sustainable, there must be an enormous and significantly radical change in the way the North Korean regime treats its own people, though not unlike the changes that South Korea made as it evolved from military dictatorship to democracy.

There would need to be proper respect for freedom of conscience, religion, and belief in both systems: Christians and adherents of other religions living in both systems should have the freedoms to believe, worship, and practise their beliefs, and to change their beliefs, that are set out in Article 18 of the Universal Declaration of Human Rights and the International Covenant on Civil and Political Rights.

The DPRK would do well to recognize that there are material benefits from promoting human rights. If religious freedom could become a reality, Christian organizations would be at liberty to act inside the Hermit Kingdom, bringing food, medicine, and education. As we have seen throughout Korean history in the last three centuries, humanitarian aid from individual Christians and church organizations has always worked towards social reform in favour of the ordinary people, with a particular bias towards the downtrodden and the suffering. Sadly, that grouping includes a vast proportion of the North Korean population.

Above all, the world wants to hear that North Korea will dismantle its prison camps and free its people. Though their existence is still denied by the DPRK regime, the camps are an unacceptable reality for the estimated 200,000 incarcerated victims, the international community, and the future state of a reunified Korea. If peace broke out on the peninsula, we would have achieved a major step towards dismantling the prison-camp network that constitutes one of North Korea's blackest stains.

All of this is achievable if only the invested powers within America, China, and South Korea have the will to do it. And if the DPRK leadership could re-engage with the South – in a form more productive than binoculars and loudhailers across a militarized border – it could surprise itself how quickly and successfully it could take the path to a remarkable modernization and re-engagement with the world which China took 30 years ago. Reconnecting the emergency North–South telephone line at Panmunjom, which was installed in 1971 and severed by the North in March 2013, would be a small but positive step.

China, by hosting a conference in Beijing, could lead its geographical and historic neighbour down the same path to a more peaceful and prosperous future.

Chapter 16

Marshall Aid for Korea

For Korea, a gradualist "two systems in one country" really is the only sensible way forward. However, there is one very recent stumbling block in the way of solving this 60-year-old problem. Many South Koreans are considerably worried about the sheer cost of reunification.

Some years ago, after Kim Dae-jung's time in office, polls showed public favour leaning towards reunification. For a while afterwards, perhaps as a backlash or in response to President Lee's Cold War rhetoric, they showed a less favourable opinion of reunification.

The 2012 race for the South Korean presidency signalled a change in the political will. All the candidates pledged a renewed dialogue with North Korea[52] and now, intriguingly, the pendulum of public opinion is swinging back again towards reunification. A 2012 poll by KBS revealed that 71 per cent of South Koreans are now in favour of reunification and 70 per cent are willing to pay the substantial costs.

Even with these positive signs, political speeches and public sentiment will not be enough to dissolve the anxiety about the cost of reunification when the time comes to pay the bill. The Korean War was an international affair and, as North Korea remains a threat to the security of many countries, the international community must step in and make a clear financial commitment to paying the costs of reunification.

In very recent history, most European powers have enjoyed the benefits of a strikingly similar policy. After the Second

52. For more, see chapter 17, "Signs of Hope".

World War, in April 1948, America created the Marshall Aid programme, which provided $13 billion of reconstruction funding over four years. Without this money, Germany – West Germany as it was – would not have been able to undergo reconstruction and it would not have become the fantastic democracy it now is.

America's goals were to rebuild a shattered Europe, remove trade barriers, modernize industry, and make Europe prosperous once more. The USA showed enormous generosity in that period. Great Britain was on its knees as a result of the war: our colonies were opting out of the Empire and everything was falling apart. And, unlike at the conclusion of the First World War, nobody was looking for reparations that would plunge nations into poverty and provide the circumstances in which the desire for revenge could fester.

By 1989, entirely thanks to the Marshall Aid programme, West Germany was in a position to roll out its own reconstruction programme in East Germany, which was to bring East Germany up to a relatively similar standard of living to the West. This prevented mass migration and also showed real generosity of spirit that proved they were deeply committed to reunification. Wounds were healed as infrastructure was rebuilt.

Reunification was the order of the day, and the same must happen in Korea.

The cost will be higher than in 1989 because the comparison between post-war Germany and Korea can only go so far. At present, the disparity between South Korea and North Korea is comparable to that between a developed country and an underdeveloped country. By contrast, East Germany, even when it was on its knees, was not the basket case that North Korea is today. There were never 3.5 million people dying of starvation and – as mentioned before – East and West Germany did not fight a war against one another with a colossal loss of life.

President Lee correctly observed that the costs involved will be enormous, which is why the international community must make an unequivocal statement to the effect that we will help with reconstruction costs. To bring this about, South Korea needs to draw up a budget for reconstructing North Korea so that the leading nations of the world can sign on the dotted line.

The message must be that a peace treaty will be quickly followed by a new Marshall Plan for Korea's reconstruction. Merely by signalling a serious intention to create a Korean Marshall Plan, the world's richest nations would help build confidence and bring about the reality of peace in Korea.

A Marshall Aid scheme for Korea, though expensive in the short term, could end the DPRK's dependence on international aid and thus help rebalance the budgets of a number of major contributing countries. China has had to invest millions of dollars' worth of resources in North Korea to keep it functioning to some degree, not to mention the cost of tens of thousands of its own soldiers' lives in the "hot" phase of the Korean War.

Between 1996 and 2005, China exported over 2 million metric tonnes of food aid to North Korea[53] and continues to provide a large percentage of all international aid to the country. This fact alone means China's commitment to a more prosperous North Korea cannot be questioned. The DPRK regime would risk total alienation by refusing to co-operate with the process. Thanks to their close history and shared Communist ideology, North Korea can have no serious objection to China backing such a programme.

Usefully, China's relationship with North Korea is not one of blind devotion. The "civilization state" has changed radically over the decades from a committed ally against the West to a partner *with* the West, providing North Korea with vital aid

---

53. Mark E. Manyin, "CRS Report for Congress – Foreign Assistance to North Korea", 26 May 2005, pp. 17, 21.

and trade. China is also wary of an unstable neighbour in the DPRK because of the all-too-permeable border between them – it is difficult to find border guards who will not take bribes. Migration from North Korea to China poses a problem on two fronts: first, it destabilizes the Chinese population and economy in the affected areas; and, second, China's policy of forced deportation back to North Korea, where concentration camps and death await the deportees, has drawn severe criticism from the international community.

North Korea is increasingly a headache that China does not need. China has as much incentive to help resolve the Korean question as any other nation invested in it, and its involvement in a Marshall Plan for North Korea would be an attractive option. With the clear commitment to a "two systems, one country" approach, the DPRK regime could not fear obliteration by being absorbed by the South and a programme of CBMs and CEMs could begin.

Realistic CBMs and CEMs could begin with something as innocuous as joint representation at international sports events under a single flag. In addition to greater glory on the medals table (as mentioned previously), joint representation at the 2012 London Olympics would also have avoided the incompetent mix-up of flags that saw the North Korean ladies' football team leave the field in Glasgow until the South Korean flag representing them was replaced by their own.

Success in joint sports events could revitalize Korean national pride and create opportunities for the single flag to be adopted in other arenas of shared public life. In a short space of time it could become as popular as the flags that have been symbolic of division for the last 60 years. It may even replace them.

CBMs and CEMs could point the way towards transforming the enormous North Korean military from a liability into a functioning limb of the future unified Korea. Joint military exercises, rather than provocative chest-beating on both sides, could bring something of the spirit of Christmas 1914 and help heal the memory of the over-long Korean cold war. The withdrawal from the entire region of American units capable of nuclear strikes would build confidence and help achieve total denuclearization of the peninsula. This in turn could lead to the partial demilitarization of both North and South.

Britain could play its part, building on the initiative of our former Chief of Defence Staff General Lord Guthrie (as detailed in chapter 14) in meeting some of the highest-ranking military figures in the DPRK. I have often urged the British Department of Defence to invite North Korean military figures to visit Sandhurst and to begin recognizing the human faces that go with the uniforms. Joint UN–Korean army manoeuvres would bring soldiers of all nations together shoulder to shoulder rather than head to head or down the sights of high-powered rifles.

Other non-threatening measures could be contributed by the likes of Britain and even by international corporations. I have campaigned vigorously to persuade the BBC to extend their World Service to the Korean peninsula. If programmes were created in the Korean language, they could be broadcast over both states in an effort to encourage social and cultural understanding between citizens of the North and South.

When I met the BBC for a preliminary discussion, they had no objections in principle but stated that budgetary restrictions were too great to expand the service to Korea. Sadly, it seems much more likely that the BBC's response was because of the British government's concern that broadcasting the BBC World Service in North Korea might hinder our engagement with the DPRK. This is, in fact, a disingenuous position to take, especially, as Daily NK journalist Chris Green rightly pointed out, because "the BBC never shied away from broadcasting into the former USSR or China for fear of putting diplomatic relations at risk in those places".[54]

As I said to Chris Green in a 2012 interview, one of the major success stories of our diplomatic relations with North Korea has been the promotion of English – it is their second language and it is now the teaching language at Pyongyang University of Science and Technology (PUST). When it comes to peace-building in North Korea, knowledge of the English language opens up the world to North Koreans, many of whom speak Chinese as well. Our language is a huge asset for North Korea in entering into an international dialogue. The BBC could play an important part in this, as could Wikipedia.

Jimmy Wales, the founder of Wikipedia, has been successful in launching the online encyclopedia in China, albeit a censored version. I understood, on meeting him, that he wants to do the same in North Korea. In addition to using language to aid forward-looking engagement with North Korea, a project such as a joint-Korean Wikipedia could help with the healing of the history of the two states as well. Moving forward, any censorship imposed by the North would be gradually eroded by the ongoing dialogue.

This approach could also heal the history of the region outside the Korean peninsula. Historians from Japan, North Korea, and South Korea could come together to begin the painful process of discussing an agreed history of the last 150 years in an effort to come to terms with their shared past, much as Germany has done in relation to purging Nazism.

This could begin today, if only the present Japanese leadership would change their provocative behaviour of publicly visiting the graves of Japanese soldiers who committed

---

54. Chris Green, "Reaping the Benefits of the BBC", Daily NK newspaper (online), 1 October 2012, www.dailynk.com/english/read. php?cataId=nk02500&num=9864

war crimes against Koreans, both North and South. Even if the Japanese government is unwilling, Japanese historians could come together with Korean historians from the North and South and together try to agree texts. And, if there were irreconcilable versions of events, the disputed texts could go together and further the conversation. Wikipedia could facilitate this and, in time, North Korean and South Korean history textbooks could contain the agreed and disputed versions of their shared history.

The acknowledgment of past crimes, such as the horrific treatment of Korean "comfort women", would enable other, ongoing, atrocities to be dealt with. The two states could do more to facilitate greater contact between families divided by the fortified 38th Parallel. The release of Southern prisoners of war, held by the North since the 1950s, would be a necessary symbolic gesture. It would do much to tear off the angry masks of distortion and bring true Korean faces to the process that could move an established peace into reunification.

Reunification *without* the approach of "two systems in one country" detailed in the previous chapter would lead to disaster. If the South tried to absorb the North, there would be massive southward migration, huge unemployment, and a power vacuum made even more dangerous by the presence of over a million unemployed North Korean soldiers. The (South) Korean economy would be destabilized and the country would collapse. Only a Marshall Plan for Korea could deflect this very real danger.

In a speech marking the 65th anniversary of Korean independence, President Lee Myung-bak proposed the creation of a reunification tax to fund a process which some analysts say would cost more than $1 trillion. This dwarfs the economic cost of German reunification. Over DM 350 billion was spent in the first three years and after 1992 it continued at DM 150 billion annually. The total of private and public money spent by West

Germany in the East, between 1990 and 1995, is put at between DM 750 and DM 850 billion – or DM 50,000 for every citizen of East Germany. Few Europeans surely would doubt today that this was a price worth paying for the tearing down of a wall that divided families, communities, and a nation.

CHAPTER 17

Signs of Hope

In late 2012, the South Korean singer "Psy" (Park Jae-sang) became the first Korean to top the British pop charts, with the quirky dance track "Gangnam Style". At the same time, North Korea's Vice-Foreign Minister, Pak Kil-yon, was addressing the United Nations General Assembly. He described the Korean peninsula as "the world's most dangerous hotspot" and said that the deteriorating situation there could "set off a thermonuclear war".

Psy became an internet phenomenon with his "imaginary horse" dance routine, quickly clocking up a staggering 700 million views[55] on YouTube. Mr Pak Kil-yon received no such attention, but the world would be foolish to ignore his dire warnings. We owe it to the people of North Korea to pay attention to their situation and to speak out more clearly on their behalf.

If we do not do so, it could have catastrophic results on a peninsula where a failure to find a long-term political settlement could one day replicate or even exceed the horrendous haemorrhaging of lives in the last Korean War.[56]

Beyond the entertaining choreography of the Gangnam dancers, and in contrast to the dark theatrics of the DPRK spokesmen, there are many mundane human tragedies unfolding every day that gain no media attention whatsoever. They never secure 1.2 billion online views or get to deliver a speech at the General Assembly but they remain the most

---

55. As of February 2013.
56. An estimated 3 million people died in the conflict.

important reason why the international community needs to do more to end the Korean War and secure a lasting peace. After 60 weary years, the conflict has long exceeded its sell-by date. The issue of human rights and their violations deserves to be the world's number-one priority.

Three days before Mr Pak Kil-yon issued his dire warning, I stood on the banks of the River Tumen, which marks the border between North-East China and North Korea. It is here that Korea's tragedy continues to be enacted every day.

For many desperate North Koreans, their attempts to leave the country end in death down the sights of a DPRK sniper's rifle. If there truly are "terrifying and dangerous hotspots" on the Korean peninsula, then surely one is the bloodied waters of the rivers that mark North Korea's borders. Equally terrifying places must be the gulags and prison camps in which the UN says 400,000 have died in the past 30 years, and where 200,000 people remain imprisoned.

The rarely used bridge at Tumen, which connects the two countries, reminds me of another symbol of the harsh divisions of the Cold War: Berlin's Checkpoint Charlie. In August 1962, an East German boy called Peter Fechter, just a couple of years older than me at the time, was shot in the pelvis by East German border guards as he attempted to escape to the West. He was left bleeding on the wire for an hour, and the press images of his body became a symbol of the sheer futility of the wall and the ideology it represented.

Ultimately, it wasn't the nuclear threat or the accompanying doomsday rhetoric that ended the Cold War. It was outrage at the systematic abuse of human rights coupled with confidence-building measures that brought leaders face to face in talks, rather than nose to nose in the deadly test of military and nuclear supremacy. The result was a previously unimaginable change in the course of twentieth-century history.

Mr Pak Kil-yon was the first North Korean minister to address the General Assembly after Kim Jong-un came to power following the death of his father, Kim Jong-il, in December 2011.

The speech was full of anger, false outrage, and rhetoric – with the traditional anti-American tirade and far-fetched claims that the US is planning a new war on the peninsula. Special hatred was reserved for the South Korean government of Lee Myung-bak, with the comment: "History will bring them to justice." Even taking into account Lee's dismal record, this is a particularly ironic exaggeration coming from a country that shoots its own citizens.

Mr Pak's speech was a lost opportunity to tell the General Assembly about some of the opportunities that offer the North the chance for peaceful change. Instead of giving a speech full of hate, he could have told the world about the new economic reforms that his country has announced – including two joint economic zones with China, brokered by Kim Jong-un's uncle, Jang Sung-taek. These zones[57] will provide long-overdue opportunities for North Koreans to legally earn a wage and support their families without having to become illegal escapees. This is undoubtedly a step in the right direction.

He could have highlighted Kim Jong-un's recent speeches promising to ease suffering among the people, or announced the new right of farmers to keep between a third and a half of their produce (modelled on the early Chinese agricultural reforms of the 1970s). These welcome developments will boost agricultural output and food supplies, help cap rising food prices, and ease malnutrition.[58]

The General Assembly would also have been pleased to hear of the new emphasis being placed on scientific and

57. Hwanggumphyong and Wihwado Economic Zone and the Rason Economic Trade Zone.
58. North Korea requires about 5 million tonnes of grain and potatoes each year to feed its people but since the early 1990s the annual harvest has been around 3.5 to 4.7 million tonnes.

technological education and the raising of the school leaving age. During 2012 students were ordered out of their universities to repair damage caused by natural disasters, to work in the fields, or to make the country ready for a national holiday. The new leadership knows that this was a mistake. It caused unrest among students by disrupting their education and it damaged the future development of the country.

Though it may come as a surprise, there are more and more encouraging signs of hope for change.

As the regime's new dictator, Kim Jong-un spent much of 2012 working to establish his grip on power and to present himself to the world as the DPRK's highest authority. He might have chosen to present himself in the image of his father – distanced, unreachable, and intimidating. However, he sought to define a different image of himself – pictured with his young wife – trying to connect with the day-to-day concerns of the people.

He showed his awareness of publicity when, in a country where parents struggle to feed their children, he was photographed at a Pyongyang zoo feeding animals. He responded by changing his behaviour and was later pictured holding a baby and inspecting food production. These are small but hopeful signs for a people who have been starved of hope as well as food.

Change came to South Korea, too, in the form of electioneering in the run-up to the December ballots. Encouragingly, before the votes were cast, all three of the South Korean presidential candidates signalled their intention to initiate new dialogue with the North. On 4 October 2012, the *Korean Times* reported that Democratic presidential candidate Moon Jae-in proposed that his administration would revitalize activity at the joint DPRK–ROK industrial complex at Kaesŏng and use it as "a starting point for his key South–North economic alliance program[me]". Most encouragingly, the *Korean Times* journalist reported that Mr Moon's plan "aims to gradually merge the economies of the two countries before full-fledged unification takes place".[59]

On the same day, the incumbent President Lee Myung-bak said that South Korea posed no actual security threat to North Korea, despite recent posturing and talk of military reform and modernization for the ROK army. "There is no country in the world that threatens North Korea. We have no intention whatsoever to subvert the North's system or seek unification through absorption,"[60] said Prime Minister Kim Hwang-sik, reading a speech on behalf of the president and – interestingly – echoing the tenets of Kim Dae-jung's Sunshine Policy. He continued: "Genuine threats to North Korea do not come from the outside, but from within."

The wounds of the recent past came closer to being healed on 28 September 2012, when Park Geun-hye, daughter of dictator General Park Chung-hee, offered an apology to those who had suffered under her father's rule. "I understand that the end does not justify the means," Ms Park said, as reported by *The Economist*; "I apologize to the victims hurt by my father's dictatorial rule in this regard."[61]

It is unclear whether a new period of Sunshine will spontaneously break out, but the two states appear to be warming to each other. On 11 October 2012, *The Times* newspaper printed a very encouraging piece on how both North and South Korea are looking to the example of Ireland in an attempt to pursue peace and reconciliation. The Good Friday Agreements and surrounding negotiations could provide a worthy model for achieving a workable peace. As *Times* journalists Leo Lewis

59. "Liberal candidates focus on N. Korea reconciliation, Jeolla support", *Korean Times*, 4 October 2012, http://www.koreatimes.co.kr/www/news/nation/2012/10/116_121493.html
60. "S. Korea poses no threat to North: president", MySinchew.com, 4 October 2012, http://www.mysinchew.com/node/78338?tid=37
61. "Sorry for the dictatorship part", *The Economist* website, http://www.economist.com/blogs/banyan/2012/09/south-koreas-presidential-race

(Beijing) and Richard Lloyd Parry (Tokyo) reported: "The example of Ireland" might show the way to ending "60 years of confrontation across the world's most militarized border." According to the two journalists, officials in Pyongyang and Seoul are "actively studying the Good Friday Agreement and the technical accords... towards resolving the world's last Cold War conflict".[62]

Such signs are hopeful indeed.

There are other causes for hope outside Korea. It seems that China no longer perceives North Korea as a buffer state against the world, and is increasingly showing an awareness of the importance of pursuing peace and protection for civilian lives. China has even participated in the international sanctions against North Korea which made it more difficult for Pyongyang to acquire technology for its missile programme. As part of this, China did not block a UN declaration condemning the North Korean attempts at launching a satellite-carrying rocket.

China's interest in making North Korea a sustainable state brings with it hope for improved living conditions for North Korea's citizens. Chinese analysts see change in North Korea as necessary in order to save the country rather than to promote unification.[63]

Other nations are finding new ways of engaging with North Korea for mutual benefit. France, after decades of refusing diplomatic contact with the DPRK leadership, has opened a Bureau of Cooperation in Pyongyang. Though this office does not constitute an embassy, it is a positive step.

Russia has also taken steps to secure an agreement with

62. Leo Lewis (Beijing) and Richard Lloyd Parry (Tokyo), "North and South Korea select model for how to get along... Ireland", *The Times,* 11 October 2012.
63. "China Analysis: Gaming North Korea", European Council on Foreign Relations, September 2012.

Pyongyang for the construction of a gas pipeline across North Korea. Only 700 kilometres separate Russia's gas supply from its would-be customer South Korea. North Korea has historically denied its enemy, South Korea, access to this source of energy. If such a pipeline is built, relations between these three states will be greatly improved.

I have taken part in Britain's engagement with North Korea – accompanied on three visits to the DPRK by Lady Cox. We have taken with us the human rights campaigners James Mawdsley and Ben Rogers, Mark Rowland, who worked for Jubilee Campaign, and the barrister, and member of the Conservative Party's Human Rights Commission, Sam Burke.

The All-Party Group has facilitated visits to Westminster by North Korean Workers Party officials and has also held open sessions with two of the DPRK's ambassadors – organized by its pro bono clerk, Mr Keith Bennett. We also held sessions with Anti-Slavery International, Christian Solidarity Worldwide, Amnesty International, members of the South Korean National Assembly, North Koreans who have given their testimonies, a South Korean doctor who works with North Korean patients in the joint Kaesŏng industrial zone, the World Food Programme, and many other organizations. All these sessions represented chances for the DPRK to hear from the world.

In the spring of 2011, as the Chair of the All-Party Group on North Korea, I received a delegation from the DPRK headed by North Korea's Speaker, Choe Tae-bok. Though the visit included a number of cordial engagements, such as going to Poet's Corner and presenting Speaker Choe with a copy of Byron's poetic works, we were able to challenge the visiting delegation on North Korea's human rights record.

During meetings with speakers and members from both Houses, there were frank and extended discussions about human rights and how international transparency on human rights issues would immediately transform North Korea's relationship with democratic nations.

At the meetings with colleagues from the Northern Ireland Assembly and the reformed paramilitaries, both parties were able to tell the North Korean delegation about their experience of reconciliation and peace-building in significant detail. The delegation also had a session with the Centre for Opposition Studies – an unusual concept in North Korea, where there is no opposition.

The delegation also witnessed Prime Minister's Question Time in the House of Commons. Afterwards, one of the North Korean delegates told me, with a trace of humour, that the Supreme People's Assembly was probably not ready for such a format yet.

The visit of Choe Tae-bok and his delegation reinforced my view that we need to open up as many lines of communication as possible with North Korea. In doing so, we must not be afraid to refuse to overlook human rights or security questions. And we must also accept that this hard-headedness can generate some hostility; one recent diplomat in London told me that he regarded our approach as "hateful" and not based on friendship. We agreed to differ, and the engagement goes on regardless.

My visits to the DPRK with Baroness Caroline Cox have borne some fruit, though I do not wish to exaggerate this. I am especially pleased, however, with progress made in the field of education and language, which I detail in the next chapter. I have also agreed to be the British patron of a proposed Pyongyang English Literary Festival, which, if held, will be the first ever English-language literary festival to be staged in the DPRK. Speaker Choe, drawn by his personal interest in poetry, has agreed to be the North Korean patron of the festival.

The programme will include discussions and workshops designed to bring authors, playwrights, scholars, and film-makers from the UK and the DPRK into direct dialogue. One of the more daring sessions will be entitled "Literature and the English Sense of Humour" and will see actors present a selection of comic scenes from Shakespeare to explore what makes people laugh. The question is this: will the timeless nature of humour be able to cross national and linguistic boundaries? In making such a cultural offering, the hope would be to encourage a greater understanding and appreciation of British culture among DPRK public audiences, and vice versa.

None of this, though, should lull us into believing that such exchanges alone are enough, and it would be exceedingly naïve not to foresee how such initiatives could be misrepresented or manipulated. Yet the alternative of doing nothing is simply a recipe for another 60 years of dangerous "brinkmanship" and a more hostile, reactive DPRK.

On 11 January 2010, the North Korean Foreign Minister Pak Ui-chun issued a remarkable statement calling for peace talks with the United States of America. In his statement, he said:

> *The denuclearization of the Peninsula is the goal of the policy consistently pursued by the Government of the Republic with a view to contributing to peace and security in North-east Asia and the denuclearization of the world... It is our conclusion that it is necessary to pay primary attention to building confidence between the DPRK and the United States, the parties chiefly responsible for the nuclear issue, in order to bring back the process for the denuclearization of the Korean Peninsula on track. If confidence is to be built between the DPRK and the US, it is essential to conclude a peace treaty for terminating the state of war, a root cause of the hostile relations, to begin with.*

> *When the parties are in the state of war where they level guns at each other, distrust in the other party can never be wiped out and the talks themselves can never make smooth*

progress, much less realizing the denuclearization. Without settling such essential and fundamental issues as war and peace no agreement can escape from frustration and failure as now...

The conclusion of the peace treaty will help terminate the hostile relations between the DPRK and the US and positively promote the denuclearization of the Korean Peninsula at a rapid tempo. Upon authorization, the DPRK Foreign Ministry courteously proposes to the parties to the Armistice Agreement (AA) an early start of the talks for replacing the AA by the peace treaty this year which marks the lapse of 60 years since the outbreak of the Korean War. The above-mentioned talks may be held either at a separate forum as laid down in the September 19 Joint Statement or in the framework of the Six-Party Talks for the denuclearization of the Korean Peninsula like the DPRK–US talks now under way in view of their nature and significance. The removal of the barrier of such discrimination and distrust as sanctions may soon lead to the opening of the Six-Party Talks.

If the parties to the AA sincerely hope for peace and security and the denuclearization of the Peninsula, they should no longer prioritize their interests but make a bold decision to deal with the fundamental issue without delay.[64]

Regrettably, the United States rejected the proposal but, as Ambassador Clifford Hart told me, the president has given him a mandate to make strenuous efforts to keep dialogue alive. Too often, though, this has been a story of missed opportunities mired in accusations of bad faith. We should be fearful lest our failure to find a way through should bring catastrophic consequences.

---

64. DPRK statement, 11 January 2011 – http://www.korea-dpr.com/forum/?p=422

As one observer told us, "If your adversary offers to talk, it is morally wrong to refuse... The North Koreans are eager for outside contact. It is not self-isolation – we are isolating them."

As recently as 1 January 2013, in his first televised New Year's Day address, Kim Jong-un was right in his assertion that "past records of inter-Korean relations show that confrontation between fellow countrymen leads to nothing but war." In a similar vein, the Republic of Korea's new President, Park Geun-hye, has called for deeper engagement. She said: "While we cannot allow the North to develop nuclear weapons... we must keep open the possibility of dialogue, including humanitarian aid."

It would be a tragedy if this tentative exploration of a new paradigm were scuppered by the third nuclear test. North Korea is at a crossroads and its traditional allies have raised the stakes in urging them to cross the bridge rather than blow it up. At the UN Security Council the Russian ambassador, Vitaly Churkin, spelt out the consequences: "Our position is that the North Korean rocket launch is a violation of a UN Security Council resolution, so the council should react."

Even more significantly, China dealt Pyongyang a significant diplomatic blow by supporting the resolution censuring North Korea for its December 2012 rocket launch and said it will withdraw its economic support if North Korea insists on proceeding with its nuclear programme.

The stakes are higher than ever and we cannot afford to miss any more opportunities. Unlike the Middle East, this is a conflict waiting to be resolved. It's time for North Korea to come in from the cold.

CHAPTER 18

The Wisest Investment

During my earlier trips to North Korea I visited the excellent English language department at Kim Il-sung University, as well as other schools in Pyongyang. Whatever differences there may be in ideology, or in the fierce arguments about human rights or security, any visitor meeting the bright young people in these institutions would surely want the best possible outcome for them and their families.

If Korea is to experience the joy of reunification, much will depend on the actions and influence of foreign powers. Yet much will also be determined by the actions of North and South Koreans in bringing about the social change necessary for a "Korean Spring".

If these young students I visited ever got the opportunity to learn about Mahatma Gandhi, they might agree with his statement that: "You must be the change you want to see in the world." It is more likely that they will have learned about Confucius's advice to anyone who wants to see change: "To put the world in order, we must first put the nation in order; to put the nation in order, we must first put the family in order; to put the family in order, we must first cultivate our personal life; we must first set our hearts right."

The key to creating cultural and political change is education. The education of the citizen should not be about propaganda or indoctrination; instead, it should equip students to reach beyond simple academic attainment and learn to think, enquire, debate, and understand how decisions will affect their lives and the future of their nation. If North Korean students have a hope of changing their country for the better, they must be aware of the ethical dilemmas, technological challenges, and cultural shifts that will result in properly engaging with the world and with their Southern neighbours. They will face problems of hunger, climate change, and the exploitation of finite resources, among many more.

A cold, detached education will not be enough – they will need an overarching moral story to guide them in learning how the individual and the state interact with the world. Knowledge alone will not immunize the next generation of scientists, engineers, and politicians against the kind of moral dysfunction that led to the outrageous human rights abuses the Korean peninsula has witnessed over the last century. It is a chilling thought that more than half of the participants in Hitler's 1942 Wannsee Conference, which planned the "final solution to the Jewish question", were either medical practitioners or in receipt of other academic doctorates. Nazi collaborators included a cast of scientists, doctors, judges, lawyers, philosophers, and academics. History must not be allowed to repeat itself.

Einstein asserted that the misuse of science could be countered only "by those who are thoroughly imbued with the aspiration toward truth and understanding… I cannot conceive of a genuine scientist without that profound faith". Creating a space for matters of faith must surely be a central objective in education.

In 2011 I had the chance to give a lecture to 600 North Korean students at the Pyongyang University of Science and Technology (PUST). The lecture was entitled "Educating for Good Science and Good Ethics: Educating for Virtue". It aroused a great deal of interest from the students, which served to remind me of the gentle power of introducing honest, robust debate in a closed society such as North Korea.

Amid the suffocating propaganda of North Korea, PUST

is a unique space in which a more complete education can be sought and found. The story of PUST is truly remarkable and gives some hope for how the future could look for North Korea.

PUST was founded by Dr James Chin-kyung Kim, the extraordinary South Korean who is North Korea's first and only honorary citizen – his certificate is number 001. He said, "I believe in the power of education: education can plant seeds of the values that are critical in reaching our desired end. These values include understanding; respect; sacrifice; and reconciliation." Dr Kim holds that good leadership is dependent on personal transformation and believes that political life needs to revolve around the concept of service, not power.

I first met Dr Kim after an old friend, Alan Godson, asked me whether I had come across his friend James Kim, who had started a university in North Korea. "No," I replied "and you must be mistaken. It must be *South* Korea. You can't start universities in North Korea." But Dr Kim has – and in doing so he has achieved the miraculous. Alan had been at theology college in Bristol with James Kim 50 years earlier and he assured me it was true. Intrigued, I asked the British ambassador, Peter Hughes, if he had come across James Kim or his university. "Yes," he said, "the whole diplomatic corps here in Pyongyang has heard about it but the authorities will not let us go there."

On my next visit, I asked the North Korean Speaker, Choe Tae-bok, whether we might go and see PUST. The following day Baroness Cox, Ambassador Hughes, and I were greeted at the campus by Dr Kim. I returned a year later in 2011 to participate in the university's first international conference. The conference delegates were an unlikely cast, including a United States astronaut, a Nobel Laureate, and a former White House adviser involved in the 1972 Mao–Nixon encounter, and our subject matter ranged from information technology to life sciences, scientific diplomacy, pollution measurement, and genetic programming, as well as my own address on science and ethics.[65]

But the eclectic cast and the unlikely programme could never be more astonishing than the simple fact that we were in North Korea, attending the country's first ever international conference on science and technology. Even this was not as incredible as the realization that the venue – the one-year-old Pyongyang University of Science and Technology – was simultaneously "international" and "private" in a country where even the lives of its citizens are treated as the property of the government.

Using education to foster mutual understanding is not a new idea. During the Cold War, America conducted many scientific exchanges with the Soviet Union, just as it did following Nixon's encounters with Mao and Zhou Enlai in 1972. The formidable challenges currently facing humanity – disease, food security, climate change, space exploration, and energy – could all provide endless opportunities for engagement with North Korean scientists.

Dr Kim has a remarkable story of his own, which only adds to the symbolic power of PUST. In 1950, at the outbreak of the Korean War, James Kim was just 15 years old when he enlisted and fought for the South against the North. One night on the battlefield, after reading John's Gospel, he promised "to God to work *with* the Chinese and the North Koreans, our enemies... I would devote my life to their service, to peace and to reconciliation". Of 800 men in his unit, so he says, just he and 16 others survived.

Between the end of the war and the start of the 1980s, Kim travelled the world. He moved between Europe, America, and

65. http://davidalton.net/2011/09/26/educating-for-good-science-and-good-ethics-educating-for-virtue-lecture-at-pyongyang-university-of-science-and-technology-north-korea-october-2011/

South Korea, working, studying, and starting businesses, but he never forgot his promise. When the time was right, he sold his businesses and his home in order to finance the setting up of a university college in South Korea. The project was a success, and by 1992 he was ready to export his model of education to China. There he established Yanbian University of Science and Technology (YUST), which was the country's first foreign joint-venture university. It was to become a model for his university in Pyongyang.

Before PUST could become a reality, Dr Kim had to return to North Korea. When he did so he was promptly arrested, accused of being an American spy, and sent to jail to await execution. When ordered to write a will, he told his captors that they could have his body parts for medical research. Stripped as he was of all possessions and property, this was the closest he could come at the time to fulfilling his vow to give everything in the service of the North Korean people.

In his will and testament, he wrote to the US government: "I died doing things I love at my own will. Revenge will only bring more revenge and it will be an endless cycle of bitter hatred. Today, it will stop here and the hate will not see a victory. I am dying 'for the love of my country and my people'. If you take any actions for my death then my death would truly have been for nothing and for no reason."

In explaining what then occurred, James Kim told me that "the North Korean government was moved and allowed me to return to my home in China". He made no public complaints about what had happened and, only two years later, they invited him back to North Korea and "asked whether I would forget our differences and build a university for them like the one I had established in China".

He said yes, but with certain conditions. He was to choose the site of the university; be given full ownership of the land; be allowed to bring in foreign professors to teach; and be authorized to establish a research and development centre.

His demands were all met and, by unbelievable coincidence or yet another miracle, the site he chose later proved to have extraordinary significance for Korea. On that site had once stood the church built to commemorate the work of the Welsh missionary Robert Jermain Thomas, who, as we have seen, was central to the story of Christianity in Korea. The church, which pre-dated the tragic division of the two Koreas, was destroyed by the Japanese during their occupation and was symbolic in many ways of Korean suffering. Dr Kim believes it was "the hand of God bringing two histories together".

Dr Kim believes his own experience is evidence that the Korean situation can ultimately be transformed through education – which "has the power to transcend nationalistic boundaries and promote cross-cultural understanding and respect". Dr Kim recognizes that change will not happen overnight and "peace comes with a price". As a childhood friend said of him, "He is neither foolish nor naïve but rather shrewd, precise, resourceful, and witty. His appetite and thirst are generated from his ideals and sense of justice."

Dr Kim and his university represent the incremental change in a country strangled by its own policies of *Songun* and *Juche*. Because of PUST, North Korea's best-educated citizens have come to value change that places the characteristics of "a prosperous future" and "a dignified future" before military might.

It remains North Korea's first and only privately funded international institution, with a small cohort of academic staff drawn from Europe, China, and North America, openly promoting a strategy for enabling North Korea's citizens to engage successfully in the world economy and global society. Amazingly, PUST has been embraced as a flagship by the DPRK leadership. If that was not enough, on 25 August 2011 Dr Kim had honorary citizenship conferred on him by the DPRK "for his extraordinary contribution to the nation's prosperity" – quite a turnaround from the death sentence passed on him earlier.[66]

Eventually, Dr Kim wants to see an industrial park created around the PUST campus, providing a springboard for international companies. Ben Rosen, the American venture capitalist and founder of Compaq Computer Corporation, has visited the campus and believes that PUST will give its students "a window to the outside world and will create a new generation of technocrats with the potential to lead future governments".

PUST's small corps of teachers, who include young men and women from England, along with Chinese, Canadians, and American Koreans, are committed to ushering in North Korea's "information age", providing English-language studies which will link its coming generation to global society. Courses take place in information technology, industry and management, and agriculture, food, and life sciences. Two more will follow – architecture and engineering, and public health.

If PUST is a window onto the world, it is also a window for the world to see into Korea, which will help introduce the kind of Confidence-Building Measures that will painstakingly and patiently help North Korea to take its place as a welcome member of the world community.

Conscious of the historic opportunity that PUST represents, Dr Kim opened the PUST International Conference by remarking that "this is a time when science can make a great difference to the future of the world's people. Through advanced science, great breakthroughs in technology, medicine, engineering and agriculture, we are overcoming past obstacles to develop economic and political stability."

66. Reminiscent, too, of the honour conferred on Matteo Ricci by the Chinese 400 years ago.

Here, then, is a good-news story from North Korea and one which does, indeed, deserve to be more widely known. One thing is abundantly clear to me. If we are reluctant to support this initiative and, through lack of resources, allow it to fail, it will represent a colossal mistake and a betrayal of a man whose vision should inspire us all.

Chapter 19

To Begin is Half the Task

In 2009, with the death of Kim Dae-jung, Korea was robbed of its greatest modern statesman, and the world lost a remarkable peacemaker. During his life, he received international acclaim, winning the Nobel Peace Prize in 2000 and the nickname "Asia's Mandela" for his lifelong devotion to peace and reconciliation in Korea. When he ran for president in 1997, the real Mandela sent him a present of the wristwatch the South African statesman had worn during the long years he suffered in prison in the name of political freedom.

Like Mandela, Kim Dae-jung lived in the belief that forgiveness is the starting point for the healing of society. As a man of deep Christian faith, he also valued justice, and very often he expressed a faith in God which was tied up with what he called the "justice of history". The following words are from his Nobel Peace Prize lecture:

> Another faith is my belief in the justice of history. In 1980, I was sentenced to death by the military regime. For six months in prison, I awaited the execution day. Often, I shuddered with fear of death. But I would find calm in the fact of history that justice ultimately prevails. I was then, and am still, an avid reader of history. And I knew that in all ages, in all places, he who lives a righteous life dedicated to his people and humanity may not be victorious, may meet a gruesome end in his lifetime, but will be triumphant and honoured in history; he who wins by injustice may dominate the present day, but history will always judge him to be a shameful loser. There can be no exception.

Kim Dae-jung held that we begin building a civil society by our own actions towards one another – by our willingness to serve rather than to dominate and by our willingness to embrace values that run counter to those which may prevail throughout mainstream society.

Kim Dae-jung said that his politics flowed from his Christian beliefs, insisting that "the Christian life is not defined by psychological phenomena" but by how we act:

> We have to be reborn every day and make fresh progress every day. The object of our conquest is ourselves. We have to fight and conquer that self that is complacent, the self that tries to escape, the self that is arrogant, and the self that is carried away by a single moment of success.

He held that everyone must learn to be generous and that "the real purpose of politics is to guarantee the rights and life of the oppressed". He also insisted that "even those who used to oppress and those who used to take things by force must be freed from their sins and allowed to participate".

I can think of no better place from which South Korea and North Korea could start.

Kim Dae-jung's message is one that all Koreans of all faiths can get behind. One of the principal mentors of Ahn Cheol-soo – the Independent candidate in the 2012 South Korean elections – was the Venerable Pomnyun Sunim, a Buddhist monk from South Korea.

During my visit to Seoul in September 2012, I had the opportunity to spend some time with him. We talked in the home of a kindly Korean woman who is at the forefront of a movement to ensure that Korean customs are kept alive. The Venerable Pomnyun and I were the recipients of a traditional Korean tea ceremony and, as we sat cross-legged, he told me why he has become one of the voices calling for a different approach to North Korea.

The decisive moment for this gentle monk came when he was on a boat on the Yalu River which separates China from North Korea. The Yalu, along with the Tumen, has been the scene of killings as North Korean border guards have opened fire on escapees. On the far side of the river he saw an emaciated child clothed in filthy rags. Having asked the steersman if they could take the boat over to the child, he was reminded that it would be an offence to enter North Korean territory and that unknown consequences could follow.

The Buddhist monk said that this experience had brought home to him the unacceptable division of Korea: "Never before had I appreciated the meaning of a border until that day," he said, adding that he felt the experience "acutely and painfully".

Up to his "Yalu Moment", Pomnyun had been sceptical about the stories of starvation and food shortages in the North. What he saw and subsequently learned about the deaths of millions, and the struggle to survive on wild roots and the bark of trees, led him to become one of the most outspoken commentators on North Korea and also the organizer of food and shelters – through his charity organization, Good Friends – for those who have managed to make it across the border into China.

As with so many other Koreans I have met, it remains this monk's ardent hope that one day the peninsula will be reunited and that never again will he have to look at a starving Korean child and be told that he may not reach out to help. It is said that the test of a nation's right to call itself civilized is how it treats its children. It must follow that a nation that kills or allows its children to die is a nation without hope. It is a thought which should concentrate the minds of Korea's leaders, both North and South.

There are other Koreans who care about reunification and who wish to banish the reality of starving children to history.

Kim Han-sol is a grandson of Kim Jong-il and the nephew of Kim Jong-un. Little was known about this young student until he found himself at the centre of a media whirlwind when the Hong Kong government denied him a visa to study there. In 2012, when attending the United World College in the city of Mostar, Bosnia-Herzegovina, Kim Han-sol re-entered the public eye when he gave a candid interview to Elisabeth Rehn, the former UN Under-Secretary-General and Special Rapporteur for Human Rights in Bosnia and Herzegovina.

Kim Han-sol appeared confident, well educated, and articulate. When Elisabeth Rehn referred to "the terrifying suffering of the people that have no food", he seemed deeply sympathetic to the plight of the North Korean people. When asked about growing up inside the country's ruling dynasty, he was keen to point out his affinity with ordinary North Korean citizens. He said:

> *I saw on both levels – in the family of the dictator and at the same time living with ordinary citizens [at my mother's house]. My parents played a big role in supporting me and telling me, "Think about the people first before you eat that food in front of you. There are a lot of people who are hungry; always think twice; be thankful for what you have."*[67]

His use of the word "dictator" to describe his grandfather Kim Jong-il was, I thought, telling of his understanding of the true state of North Korea and its people.

When asked about his dreams for the future, he talked openly about reunification and humanitarian activities:

---

67. The entire transcript can be viewed at http://lybio.net/kim-han-sol-interviewed-by-elisabeth-rehn/people/

> *I've always dreamed I will go back one day and make things better and make it easier for the people there. I also dream of reunification because it is really sad I can't go to the other side and see my friends there. My friends say, "It would be really great to take a bus to South Korea or North Korea and meet." That is one of the dreams.*

The friends to whom he refers are truly international; they include his Libyan room-mate and even some South Koreans. Encouragingly, he seemed to understand that the path to achieving his friends' simple dream is in no way simple:

> *For me, I picture myself continuing my education. After university, hopefully, I picture myself volunteering, engaging in humanitarian projects, contributing to building world peace – especially back home because that's a really important part of me that Koreans are divided and that we can, if we put in a little effort, step by step, we can come to a conclusion and be reunited. It is going to be a step-by-step process.*

An individual such as Kim Han-sol could become a useful broker in engaging the North Korean people in reconnecting with ordinary South Korean people and the international community. As a well-travelled and educated young man of the Kim dynasty, and one who appears to care deeply for humanitarian issues worldwide and in his own country, his voice would be heard more quickly and clearly by the North Korean people than that of any "outsider".

There are even powerful insiders in the DPRK's leadership who have said that reunification is the single dream of all Koreans.

When I hosted the first visit of the North Korean Speaker, Choe Tae-bok, to Westminster, part of the itinerary included a public meeting which was attended by a South Korean student.

After the main session, Ambassador Choe was approached by the young woman, who said, "Sir, you are the first North Korean I have ever met in my life, and I had to come to London to do that. Tell me – when will I be able to meet my brothers and sisters in North Korea?"

Very moved, Choe replied, "You are my daughter too. Reunification is the single most important goal for Korea."[68]

When Kim Jong-il died in 2011, North Korea expressed grief to an extent that in the West we found hard to gauge or understand. One mourner in particular interested me. Despite the history between North and South, and despite the hyperbolic nature of Kim Jong-il's personality cult, the widow of former South Korean president Kim Dae-jung crossed the closed border into North Korea to express her condolences. The 89-year-old Lee Hee-ho went with a private group of 18 mourners to reach out to the people of North Korea in the midst of what was to them a nightmarish trauma.

State media in North Korea showed Lee Hee-ho being welcomed by Kim Jong-il's son, Kim Jong-un. Had she so desired, she could have lambasted the North for its system's cruelty and tyranny. Instead, she made her remarkable journey to North Korea because she understood that an expression of condolence to the bereaved can create a rare opportunity for healing. It may achieve nothing in isolation but, as part of a larger effort of engagement, it may help thaw the freeze that has become so deep in the Korean peninsula.

The deadlock between North and South Korea cannot and will not last. It will break, for either good or bad. If we want to prevent further loss of life, and even war, we must be prepared to move first and erode the power of the dictatorship, not with weapons and threats, but with love – what some call "tough love".

68. Personal anecdote of David Alton.

William Gladstone said that the "love of power should be replaced with the power to love" and I subscribe to that philosophy, but this should not be mistaken for weakness. There are moments when one has to fight for the freedoms that we all cherish. I supported Britain's decision to arm itself when it felt threatened by the former Soviet Union, but if that was all we had done, it would have been a huge error – an historic error of great enormity. But that was *not* all we did. Likewise, it would have been another terrible mistake to continue building walls between the West and the USSR, but that is not what we did either. It was through strong defence accompanied by dialogue that the change came.

Korea can be unified in a positive, safe, and productive way to the relief and blessing of all involved, unrealistic as it might now seem. There are some events that are unimaginable until they happen – we must remember that although it took until 1989 to bring down the Berlin Wall, no one could believe it truly possible until it happened. And it did happen, even though I had often doubted, as I travelled in the former USSR, that I'd see it in my lifetime.

I've witnessed the most extraordinary changes in terrible situations, thanks to dialogue and unwavering opposition to tyranny, often led by Christians speaking up for others. I've not only seen the Berlin Wall go; I've seen apartheid disappear, which I had opposed since joining the Anti-Apartheid Association at the age of 17.

I have seen radical change in Burma, where I've been illegally three times into Karen State. After almost two decades of imprisonment and house arrest, the Burmese opposition leader Aung San Suu Kyi was finally released on 13 November 2010. She had, of course, won the 1990 election, but was denied office by the brutal military dictatorship that has waged open war against its own people. I have since been able to greet her when she came here, and, with others from my university, to present her with her honorary fellowship, the citation for which I'd given in absentia two years earlier, never believing I would actually be able to give it to her in person. Now the military junta in Rangoon is surrendering significant political power and huge steps are being made towards peace and reconciliation.

There is also the case of Northern Ireland. It was once unimaginable that Ian Paisley and Martin McGuinness could become First Minister and Deputy First Minister of the Northern Ireland Assembly. Through dialogue, we were able to find a way forward which disarmed the violent and ensured that revenge and reprisals were in no way as desirable as peace.

What seems a faraway dream can happen more quickly than one might imagine. When asked by a young MP "What determines the shape of politics?", Harold Macmillan replied, "Events, dear boy, events." And they can move much more quickly than we might sometimes anticipate. Events are already unfolding.

While I was standing at the Tumen River in late 2012, the first students from PUST were arriving in London to start their studies at Westminster College and two other Chevening scholars are at Cambridge University.[69] At Oxford, John Lee of Hertford College and from Seoul was elected as the first Korean to become president of the Oxford Union. Each of these young people represents a more hopeful future. North Koreans studying in Britain and others studying in the country's first international university can become a channel for dialogue. They represent an opportunity to move towards a peaceful future for Korea. Any one of them could be their generation's Kim Dae-jung or Cardinal Stephen Kim.

---

69. This year of study was to widen the North Korean students' cultural experience. It was not strictly an "exchange" programme because no British students were sent to PUST.

We owe it to their generation – to the North Koreans who die trying to escape across the Tumen and Yalu Rivers and those who still languish in prison camps – to take every opportunity to bring Korea closer to the dream of reunification. This requires opening up as many channels of communication as possible. We must do everything we can to saturate North Korea with goodwill. Then, when the time is right, North and South Koreans can face each other as fellow Koreans, and work towards a shared dream of a unified Korea.

To fail in this would bring us closer to the frequent and, sadly, unheeded predictions of thermonuclear war, which, if they came to pass, would reduce the whole peninsula to an irradiated cemetery.

The division of Korea into two states must be healed, and the path towards that lies in protecting and promoting human rights in a wide-ranging and robust process aimed at thawing the last outpost of the Cold War. Too many world powers have an investment in Korea to allow peace and healing to come solely from within, and the international community's engagement with Korea has often been woefully counterproductive. But there is also a wealth of international experience in peace and reconciliation which can be directly applied to this very dangerous situation of a divided and nuclear-powered Korean peninsula. What we need is another Helsinki, but with a Korean face. Building on the experience of the Helsinki Accords, the Sunshine Policy, Europe's Marshall Aid programme, and a variety of experiences from Northern Ireland to South Africa, Korea must also seize the opportunity for change. It's high time to end the war.

The Korean proverb tells us that "to begin is half the task", so, if we want to achieve peace that leads towards a unified Korea, how do we begin? With a combination of heart and head...

We must build bridges, not walls.

How to Make a Difference

Learn more:
Register at www.davidalton.net

Take action:
Write to your MP to urge action on:
- Food aid for North Korea
- The DPRK's human rights abuses
- Ending the Korean War in a peace treaty
- A renewed Helsinki-style engagement with North Korea.

Get in touch with:
Dr Marzuki Darusman, the United Nations Special Rapporteur on Human Rights in North Korea:
marzukidarusman@yahoo.com

Support the following organizations, which are mentioned in *Building Bridges* or are connected with it:

Amnesty International
www.amnesty.org.uk

Baroness Cox's Humanitarian Aid Relief Trust (HART)
www.hart-uk.org

Caritas Korea
www.caritas.or.kr/index_en.html

CSW
www.csw.org.uk

Freedom Now
www.freedom-now.org

Human Rights Watch
www.hrw.org

Jubilee Campaign
www.jubileecampaign.co.uk
www.jubileeusa.org

Liberty in North Korea (LiNK)
www.linkglobal.org

Mercy Corps
www.mercycorps.org.uk

Sant'Egidio
www.santegidio.org/en

The World Food Programme (WFP)
www.wfp.org

The World Health Organization (WHO)
www.who.int/en

US Committee for Human Rights in North Korea
www.hrnk.org

World Day Against the Death Penalty
www.hrea.org/index.php?doc_id=889

Worldwide Coalition to Stop Genocide in North Korea
www.stopnkgenocide.com

Glossary

Places

38th Parallel The boundary between North Korea and South Korea before the Korean War.

Baekdu Mountain A volcanic mountain on the border between North Korea and China; where the North Korean origin myth takes place.

Baekje kingdom Founded in 18 BC, this was the south-western kingdom in the Three Kingdoms Period of Korean history.

British Embassy in North Korea Britain and North Korea opened resident embassies in each other's capital cities on 12 December 2000. Britain has provided English language and human rights training to DPRK officials.

Chosŏn Two kingdoms in Korea: the first, founded in 2333 BC, is differentiated from the second, founded in 1392, by the prefix "ancient".

Demilitarized Zone (DMZ) Korea's DMZ is a 250-kilometre strip of heavily fortified land that separates North Korea from South Korea.

Democratic People's Republic of Korea (DPRK) The state's own term for North Korea.

Han River A major river in South Korea, which runs through Seoul. It is also the site of many occasions of martyrdom.

Helsinki The capital city of Finland, where the Conference on Security and Co-operation in Europe, aimed at improving relations with the Communist bloc, was held.

Hermit Kingdom Term applied to Korea during the Chosŏn Kingdom period because of its isolationist policies. The term is still used to describe North Korea.

Hong Kong Hong Kong is a Special Administrative Region (SAR) within China which operates two systems within one country. It provides a working model of reunification for Korea.

Incheon Site of the American landings at the end of the Second World War and the site of General Douglas MacArthur's counterstrike in the Korean War.

Juche Tower The crumbling monument to commemorate Kim Il-sung's 70th birthday.

Kaesŏng City in the south of North Korea, near to the joint North–South Kaesŏng Industrial Park.

Kaesŏng Industrial Park Set 10 kilometres inside North Korea, the Kaesŏng Industrial Park is a joint industrial park between North Korea and South Korea.

Koguryŏ kingdom Founded in 37 BC, this was the northern kingdom in the Three Kingdoms Period of Korean history.

Korean peninsula The 1,100 kilometre-long peninsula between Japan and mainland China.

Myeongdong Cathedral The Cathedral Church of the Virgin Mary of the Immaculate Conception (known as Myeongdong Cathedral) is the Roman Catholic cathedral of Seoul, South Korea.

Naktong River The natural boundary that the ROK and US forces used in establishing the Pusan Perimeter.

North Korea See DPRK.

Panmunjom An abandoned village on the border between North and South Korea where the 1953 Armistice was signed.

Pusan Now South Korea's second-largest city, Pusan was also the port to which ROK and US forces retreated in the Korean War. They established the Pusan Perimeter along the Naktong River, which they held against repeated DPRK assaults.

Pyongyang The capital city of North Korea.

Pyongyang University of Science and Technology (PUST)
North Korea's only private university. It is also a centre for excellence in North Korea.

Republic of Korea (ROK) The state in the south of the Korean peninsula. Since its creation it has undergone many transitions in power and constitutional definition, with subsequent changes to its name. These include the Second Republic of South Korea, Third Republic of South Korea and so on until the foundation of the Sixth Republic in 1987.

Seoul South Korea's capital city.

Silla kingdom Founded in 57 BC, this was the eastern kingdom in the Three Kingdoms Period of Korean history.

South Korea See Republic of Korea (ROK).

Taedong River One of North Korea's largest rivers. It runs through Pyongyang.

Tumen River A river beginning at Baekdu Mountain and terminating at the Sea of Japan. It marks the boundary between North Korea, China and Russia.

Yanbian University of Science and Technology (YUST)
A research university in the city of Yanji, Jilin Province, China.

Yeonpyeong Island On 23 November 2010, DPRK forces fired approximately 170 artillery shells and rockets at the island, killing four and injuring 19 South Koreans. South Korean forces returned fire. The incident raised the already heightened tensions between the two states.

People

Admiral Yi Sun-sin Brilliant Korean admiral famed for defeating the Japanese invasions of the late 1500s.

Ahn Cheol-soo A South Korean businessman and politician who ran in the 2012 South Korean presidential race.

Ahn Myeong-cheol North Korean defector and ex-prison guard.

Ai Weiwei An artist and critic of China's record on human rights and democracy.

Aung San Suu Kyi The Nobel Peace Prize-winning politician who won the 1990 election in Burma but was detained under house arrest by the military dictatorship until 2010.

Baroness (Caroline) Cox A cross-bench member of the House of Lords and founder of the Humanitarian Aid Relief Trust (HART), a humanitarian aid and advocacy charity.

Cardinal Stephen Kim Stephen Kim Sou-hwan was a senior Catholic cardinal and the Archbishop of Seoul, South Korea.

Chen Guangcheng Chen Guangcheng is a blind civil rights activist who took refuge in the US Embassy in Beijing after escaping house arrest imposed by Chinese authorities.

Choe Tae-bok A senior figure in the DPRK who has held a number of high-profile roles, including the chairmanship of the Supreme People's Assembly.

Chun Doo-hwan Army general and dictator who ruled South Korea between 1979 and 1988.

Comfort women Girls and women forced into sexual slavery by the Japanese army during the Second World War. Japan has refused to acknowledge its actions against these women and denies their claims.

Confucius (551 BC – 479 BC) Chinese philosopher whose system influenced many Eastern cultures and governments. His teachings emphasized both personal and governmental morality and contained tenets shared by many of the major world religions, such as the Golden Rule.

David Hawk The human rights expert and author on the subject of North Korea.

Deng Xiaoping (22 August 1904 – 19 February 1997) Leader of the Communist Party of China whose reforms led the country towards a market economy.

Desmond Tutu Desmond Mpilo Tutu is the retired Anglican Archbishop of Cape Town and a renowned opponent of apartheid. He remains a committed activist for social rights.

Divine Prince Hwanung The divine, mythical founder of the ancient Chosŏn kingdom.

Douglas MacArthur (26 January 1880 – 5 April 1964) An American army general who played a central role for the Allies in the Pacific Theatre of the Second World War. He also commanded American and International forces in the Korean War until he was relieved by General Matthew Ridgway.

Field Marshal General the Lord Guthrie of Craigiebank Field Marshal Charles Ronald Llewelyn Guthrie, Baron Guthrie of Craigiebank, is one of the United Kingdom's highest-ranking officers. He was Chief of the General Staff 1994–1997 and Chief of the Defence Staff 1997–2001.

Geoffrey Howe Richard Edward Geoffrey Howe, Baron Howe of Aberavon, was a senior Conservative politician and now speaks in the House of Lords on foreign policy issues.

Hazel Smith Professor of Security and Resilience at Cranfield University and an expert on the dangers of famine and malnutrition.

Heavenly Emperor Hwanin The Emperor of Heaven and father of Divine Prince Hwanung.

Hu Jintao President of China and senior leader in China's Communist Party. He is expected to transfer power to Xi Jinping in March 2013.

Hwang Jang-yop (17 February 1923 – 10 October 2010) The architect of *Juche* who defected in 1997. He remains the highest-ranking North Korean defector.

James Chin-kyung Kim The founder of both North Korea's Pyongyang University of Science and Technology (PUST) and China's Yanbian University of Science and Technology (YUST).

James E. Hoare Appointed British Chargé d'affaires in Pyongyang by Tony Blair, Hoare was critical of President Lee's rejection of the Sunshine Policy.

James Mawdsley James Mawdsley is a seminarian and human rights campaigner who was imprisoned and tortured in Burma after teaching English in a Burmese refugee camp.

Jang Sung-taek The uncle of Kim Jong-un and a leading figure in the DPRK government.

Jeon Young-ok A North Korean defector.

Jeong-ai Shin North Korean defector and survivor of the notorious Camp 15.

Jimmy Wales Co-founder of Wikipedia, who has worked to establish access to Wikipedia in restricted countries such as China.

Jung Guang-il North Korean defector and torture survivor.

Kim Dae-jung (3 December 1925 – 18 August 2009) South Korean President and Nobel Peace Prizewinner.

Kim Han-sol The Western-educated grandson of Kim Jong-il.

Kim Hye-sook North Korean defector and artist.

Kim Il-sung (15 April 1912 – 8 July 1994) The first leader of the DPRK, father of Kim Jong-il and grandfather of Kim Jong-un.

Kim Jae-gyu (6 March 1926 – 24 May 1980) The Director of Central Intelligence who assassinated General Park Chung-hee in 1979.

Kim Jong-il (16 February 1941 – 17 December 2011) The Supreme Leader of North Korea from 1994 to 2011.

Kim Jong-pil The founder of the (South) Korean Central Intelligence Agency.

Kim Jong-un Leader of the DPRK, son of Kim Jong-il and grandson of Kim Il-sung.

Kim Joo-il North Korean political dissident and expatriate.

Kim Song-ju Kim Il-sung's original name.

Kim Tu-bong He was Chairman of the Workers Party before Kim Il-sung.

Kim Young-sam President of South Korea from 1993 to 1998.

King Dangun The son of Divine Prince Hwanung and the legendary founder of the ancient Chosŏn people.

King Gojong/Emperor Gwangmu (8 September 1852 – 21 January 1919) King Gojong was the 26th king of the second Chosŏn dynasty who became the first emperor of the Great Korean Empire. He was forced to abdicate by the Japanese.

Lee Hee-ho The wife of Kim Dae-jung, and a political activist.

Lee Keumsoon North Korean victim of the unofficial prison camps.

Lee Myung-bak President of South Korea (2007–12), who took a harder line with North Korea, resulting in an escalation of tensions.

Lee Young-kuk North Korean defector and ex-presidential bodyguard.

Mao Zedong (26 December 1893 – 9 September 1976) The Chairman of the Central Committee of the Communist Party of China until his death.

Martin Jacques A writer, editor, and journalist who was the editor of the Communist Party of Great Britain's journal, *Marxism Today.*

Matteo Ricci (6 October 1552 – 11 May 1610) Italian Jesuit priest and missionary to China.

Pak Kil-yon North Korean diplomat.

Pak Ui-chun A North Korean diplomat and the DPRK's Minister for Foreign Affairs.

Park Chung-hee Army general and dictator of South Korea between 1961 and 1979 following a military coup. He was assassinated by Kim Jae-kyu, the director of the Korean Central Intelligence Agency.

Park Geun-hye 2012 South Korean presidential candidate and daughter of dictator General Park Chung-hee.

Park Jae-sang – "Psy" Psy is a South Korean musician and performer responsible for the record-breaking internet video of his song "Gangnam Style".

Peter Fechter (14 January 1944 – 17 August 1962) A young East German bricklayer who was shot dead while attempting to defect to the West by crossing the Berlin Wall. His death became a symbol of the futility of the division of Germany.

Queen Min Later known as Empress Myeongseong, Korean Queen Min was an outspoken critic of Japanese expansion and was murdered on 8 October 1895.

Robert Jermain Thomas Welsh missionary and evangelist who distributed Korean-language Bibles and was present at the *General Sherman* Incident.

Robert Park Human rights activist and founder of Worldwide Coalition to Stop Genocide in North Korea. He was abducted and tortured by North Korea.

Roh Moo-hyun (6 August 1946 – 23 May 2009) The President of South Korea who followed Kim Dae-jung.

Roh Tae-woo Army general and President of South Korea from 1988 to 1993.

Shin Dong-hyok A North Korean prison camp survivor and defector. He spends his time on peace-building work.

Siberian Seven The Siberian Seven took refuge in the US Embassy in Moscow to escape the USSR.

Syngman Rhee Syngman Rhee was the first President of the provisional government of the Republic of Korea in exile during the Japanese occupation. He was also the first President of South Korea and implemented ruthless policies to protect his own power.

Tony Blair Prime Minister of Great Britain (2 May 1997 – 27 June 2007). Since leaving office he has worked as the Middle East Envoy for the United Nations, European Union, United States, and Russia, and also in senior advisory capacities for JP Morgan Chase and Zurich Financial Services.

Toyotomi Hideyoshi Samurai general who invaded Korea in 1592 and 1597.

Ungnyeo The mythological bear who takes on human form and becomes the mother of the Korean people.

The Venerable Pomnyun A Buddhist monk from South Korea and commentator on North Korean human rights and aid issues.

Xi Jinping Vice-President of China and leader of China's Communist Party.

Yi Seung-hun Baptized Peter, he was one of the first Roman Catholic martyrs in Korea.

Yi Songgye General and first king of the second Chosŏn kingdom, who overthrew the Koryŏ dynasty.

Yoo Sang-joon A North Korean defector.

Yuk Young-soo (29 November 1925 – 15 August 1974) The wife of President Park Chung-hee who was killed in an assassination attempt against her husband. She was also the mother of South Korean politician Park Geun-hye.

Zhou Enlai (5 March 1898 – 8 January 1976) The first Premier of the People's Republic of China.

Other terms/events

1953 Armistice A stopgap ceasefire agreement which paused the hostilities in the Korean War. It never led to a permanent peace treaty.

1975 Helsinki Final Act of the Conference on Security and Co-operation in Europe The final act was the signing of a declaration by 35 states to improve relations between the Communist bloc and the West.

1994 Agreed Framework This agreement was designed to replace North Korea's aging nuclear reactors with less dangerous light water reactor power plants, which cannot be so easily "weaponized".

April 19 Movement The popular uprising that overthrew Syngman Rhee's government and forced his exile.

The Asian Centre for Human Rights (ACHR) The ACHR is an NGO working to promote human rights in Asia.

Cheonan ROKS *Cheonan* was a South Korean Navy corvette which was sunk by a North Korean torpedo on 26 March 2010. Forty-six of the 104 crew are still missing, presumed drowned. The DPRK regime denies responsibility.

Chosen Army The Japanese-controlled Korean Army created to repel Russian forces and put down nationalist uprisings.

Chosun Ilbo **(Korea Daily News)** The Korea Daily News was established in September 1919 and closed under Japanese occupation in 1940. The newspaper reopened after the Japanese surrender at the end of the Second World War.

Cold War Period of extreme political tension (1945–91) between the Western world powers led by the United States of America and the Communist world, led by the USSR.

Communism in Korea Before Kim Il-sung's faction achieved dominance, Korean Communism was represented by domestic Communists, who had endured the occupation in Korea; the Yenan Communists, who had fought in China with Mao Zedong against the Japanese; and the Soviet Communists, who had waged their campaign against the Japanese forces in Russian territories. Kim Il-sung had the domestic and Yenan Communists' contributions purged from party history.

Confidence-Building Measures (CBMs) CBMs are designed to improve relations through co-operation and joint exercises, sometimes involving military units.

Confidence-Enhancing Measures (CEMs) CEMs are designed to improve relations through co-operation on exclusively civilian projects and exercises.

Confucianism See Confucius.

Database Centre for North Korean Human Rights (NKDB)
The Seoul-based NKBD aims to produce unbiased information regarding North Korean human rights violations in a prompt, systematic, and organized way.

Famine of the 1990s/The Arduous March The famine in North Korea that occurred between 1994 and 1998. Estimates of deaths are between 240,000 and 3.5 million.

Fatherland Liberation War North Korea's name for the Korean War, in which they claim to have defeated the aggressor – America – and driven them out of the territory.

First Lightning nuclear device The first Russian atomic weapon, exploded on 29 August 1949, which went a long way towards tipping the power of the Cold War away from American superiority and enabled Stalin to take a more aggressive international policy based on the premise of "mutually assured destruction".

First Sino-Japanese War War fought between China and Japan (1 August 1894 – 17 April 1895) for the control of Korea.

***General Sherman* incident** The *General Sherman* was an armed American trading ship which was destroyed by Korean forces. The incident became leverage for America in negotiating for access to Korean markets.

The Great Korean Empire The name of Korea between October 1897 and the humiliating Annexation Treaty of 1910.

Hangul The native alphabet of the Korean language, invented in 1443. It is the official script of North Korea and South Korea.

Healing of history This is a process of peace and reconciliation in which countries, governments, and groups acknowledge and make amends for historic crimes. In the Korean context, Japan has much to do.

Helsinki with a Korean Face David Alton's informal manifesto for engagement with North Korea.

International Institute of the Juche Idea One of the many non-existent organizations invented by the Korean Central News Agency (KCNA) to add prestige to the DPRK regime.

Japan–Korea Annexation Treaty of 1910 The treaty that formally began the occupation of Korea.

Japanese occupation of Korea Following the Annexation Treaty of 1910, Japan occupied Korea until surrendering to the Allies on 15 August 1945.

Juche North Korea's policy of self-reliance, designed by Hwang Jang-yop and developed by Kim Il-sung and Kim Jong-il.

KCNA The Korean Central News Agency is the news portion of the DPRK's propaganda machine.

Kimilsungism-Kimjongilism A recent fusion of *Juche* and *Songun* under Kim Jong-un.

Korean War The war between the Republic of Korea and the Democratic People's Republic of Korea, 25 June 1950 – 27 July 1953, supported by their allies the US and China respectively. The war ground to a halt in 1953 with a ceasefire but never concluded in a formal peace treaty. Thus the war is still ongoing.

Korean War Abductees South Korean citizens who have been abducted by the DPRK since the Korean War. They are not acknowledged by the North Korean authorities and the issue remains a stumbling block in the way of reconciliation and reunification.

Koryŏ dynasty The Korean dynasty (918–1392), which gave its name to the Korean state.

The March First Movement One of the first displays of mass resentment by Korean citizens against occupation by Japan.

March Till They Die The title of Father Philip Crosbie's book, which tells the horrific story of North Korean treatment of religious leaders in the Korean War.

Marshall Plan Officially called the European Recovery Program (ERP), the Marshall Plan or Marshall Aid Plan poured 12,731 million dollars' worth of aid into Europe for reconstruction after the Second World War. A similar plan will be needed to reconstruct Korea if reunification is to become a viable option.

Operation Chromite US Army General Douglas MacArthur's successful operation to land a major international force on the Korean peninsula with the objective of retaking Seoul from DPRK forces.

Prison camps/Forced labour camps Though their existence is denied by the DPRK regime, an estimated 200,000 people are imprisoned in these sprawling camps, which are also sites of systematic human rights violations.

Rodong ballistic missile North Korea's longest-range ballistic missile.

Russo-Japanese War of 1904–1905 The war fought by Russia and Japan over Manchuria and Korea.

Second Sino-Japanese War The war fought by China and Japan between 7 July 1937 and 2 September 1945 which was absorbed by the wider conflict of the Second World War.

Six-Party Talks Talks involving North Korea, South Korea, the USA, China, Japan, and Russia aimed at resolving the security issues raised by North Korea's nuclear programme.

Songun North Korea's policy of "military first", which prioritizes defence funding above all other needs – at the expense of the starving population.

The Sunshine Policy Kim Dae-jung's policy of soft power designed to improve relations with North Korea through incentives and goodwill. It took its name from a fable by Aesop.

Task Force Smith A small force of poorly equipped American soldiers who first engaged the DPRK army in the Korean War.

Treaty on the Non-Proliferation of Nuclear Weapons The international treaty for the regulation and denuclearization of the world through peaceful co-operation. Opened for signature in 1968, North Korea signed it on 12 December 1985.

Unit 731 – the "Epidemic Prevention and Water Purification Department" Unit 731 was a unit of the Imperial Japanese Army responsible for a catalogue of war crimes and human rights violations in the form of experimentation on live subjects and weapons-testing on civilian targets.

Wikipedia Wikipedia is a user-edited online encyclopedia that has an important role to play in the free movement of information and agreeing history.

World Day Against the Death Penalty The World Coalition Against the Death Penalty is an alliance of NGOs and other organizations which organizes the annual event on 10 October.

The World Food Programme (WFP) A branch of the United Nations and the world's second-largest humanitarian organization, which addresses hunger.

The World Health Organization (WHO) A specialized agency of the United Nations (UN) for international public health.

Yushin Restoration/Constitution A South Korean self-coup in October 1972 in which President Park Chung-hee assumed dictatorial powers and drew up a new constitution.

Further Reading

Philip Crosbie, *March Till They Die*, Newman Press, 1956.

Bruce Cumings, *The Origins of the Korean War*, Princeton University Press, 1992.

Bruce Cumings, *Korea's Place in the Sun: A Modern History*, W. W. Norton & Co. Ltd, 2005.

Barbara Demick, *Nothing to Envy: Real Lives in North Korea*, Granta Books, 2010.

Aidan Foster-Carter, *Korea's Coming Reunification: Another East Asian Superpower?*, Economist Intelligence Unit, 1992.

Blaine Harden, *Escape from Camp 14: One Man's Remarkable Odyssey from North Korea to Freedom in the West*, Mantle, 2012.

Max Hastings, *The Korean War*, Pan, 2010.

David Hawk, *Pursuing Peace While Advancing Rights: The Untried Approach to North Korea*, 2010.

David Hawk, *The Hidden Gulag*, US Committee for Human Rights in North Korea.

Kang Chol-Hwan, Pierre Rigoulot, and Yair Reiner, *The Aquariums of Pyongyang: Ten Years in the North Korean Gulag*, Atlantic Books, 2006.

Kim Dae-jung, *Prison Writings*, University of California Press, 1987.

Kim Dae-jung, *Nobel Lecture*, The Nobel Foundation, 2000.

Mike Kim, *Escaping North Korea: Defiance and Hope in the World's Most Repressive Country*, Rowman & Littlefield, 2010.

Lee Hee-ho, *Praying for Tomorrow (Letters to My Husband in Prison)*, University of Southern California, 2000.

B. R. Myers, *The Cleanest Race*, Melville House, 2012.

Ongoing Tragedy – Testimonies of the Korean War Abductees' Families, Seoul: Korean War Abduction Research Institute, 2012.

Hazel Smith, *Reconstituting Korean Security: A Policy Primer*, United Nations University Press, 2007.

Young-bok Yoo (author) and Paul T. Kim (translator), *Tears of Blood: A Korean POW's Fight for Freedom, Family, and Justice*, Korean War POW Affairs – USA, 2012.

Index